ALSO BY MICHAEL IGNATIEFF

Non-Fiction

A Just Measure of Pain:
The Penitentiary in the Industrial Revolution, 1750-1850

The Needs of Strangers

The Russian Album

Blood and Belonging:
Journeys into the New Nationalism

The Warrior's Honor:
Ethnic War and the Modern Conscience

Isaiah Berlin:
A Life

Virtual War:
Kosovo and Beyond

The Rights Revolution

Human Rights as Politics and Idolatry

Fiction

Aysa
Scar Tissue

Michael Ignatieff

EMPIRE LITE

Nation-building in Bosnia,
Kosovo and Afghanistan

VINTAGE

Published by Vintage 2003

2 4 6 8 10 9 7 5 3 1

Copyright © Michael Ignatieff 2003

Michael Ignatieff has asserted his right under the Copyright, Designs
and Patents Act 1988 to be identified as the author of this work

First published in Great Britain in 2003 by Vintage

Vintage
Random House, 20 Vauxhall Bridge Road,
London SW1V 2SA

Random House Australia (Pty) Limited
20 Alfred Street, Milsons Point, Sydney,
New South Wales 2061, Australia

Random House New Zealand Limited
18 Poland Road, Glenfield,
Auckland 10, New Zealand

Random House (Pty) Limited
Endulini, 5A Jubilee Road, Parktown 2193,
South Africa

The Random House Group Limited Reg. No. 954009
www.randomhouse.co.uk

A CIP catalogue record for this book
is available from the British Library

ISBN 0 099 45543 9

Typeset by Palimpsest Book Production Limited,
Polmont, Stirlingshire
Printed and bound in Great Britain by
Cox & Wyman Limited, Reading, Berkshire

Contents

Preface

Since 1993 I have been reporting on ethnic war, the collapse of old states and the fiery birth of new ones. Three books have resulted from my travels to zones of conflict: *Blood and Belonging*, *The Warrior's Honor* and *Virtual War*. *Empire Lite* is the fourth in the series. Unlike the others, which focused on the dynamics of ethnic conflict and the dilemmas of intervention, this one deals with the imperial struggle to impose order once intervention has occurred. It is focused on the conflict at the heart of the nation-building enterprise everywhere, between the imperial interests of the intervening powers, chiefly the Americans, and the local interests of the people and their leadership to rule themselves. The essential paradox of nation-building is that temporary imperialism – empire lite – has become the necessary condition for democracy in countries torn apart by civil war.

The book was written with an invasion of Iraq in prospect. If it occurs, an imperial occupation of the country will follow and the dilemmas of nation-building described in these pages will recur in especially stark form.

Three of the essays in this book first appeared in the *New York Times Magazine*. I wish to thank Kyle Crichton and Gerry Marzorati for commissioning them and also thank all the people I met on the road who helped me try to figure out what was going on. As always, the book is dedicated to the one who stayed at home, making everything possible, my wife, Suzanna Zsohar.

Michael Ignatieff
London, January 2003

Introduction

We live in a world that has no precedent since the age of the later Roman emperors. It is not just the military domination of the world by a single power. Nor is it even the awesome reach of this capability, for example, having an air-command centre in Saudi Arabia able to order B52 strikes on a mountain top in Afghanistan, within seventeen minutes of receiving target coordinates from Special Forces on the ground. Nor is it just the display of resolve. Empires that do not demonstrate inflexible determination do not survive. Terrorists everywhere have been cured of the illusion, created by the American retreat from Somalia in 1993, that the empire lacks the stomach for a fight. The Roman parallels are evident, with the difference that the Romans were untroubled by an imperial destiny, while the Americans have had an empire since Teddy Roosevelt, yet persist in believing they do not.

True, there are no American colonies and American corporations do not need their governments to acquire territory by force in order to acquire markets. So the new empire is not like those of times past, built on colonies and conquest. It is an empire lite, hegemony without colonies, a global sphere of influence without the burden of direct administration and the risks of daily policing. It is an imperialism led by a people who remember that their country secured its independence by revolt against an empire, and who have often thought of their country as the friend of anti-imperial struggles everywhere. It is an empire, in other words, without consciousness of itself as such. But that does not make it any less of an empire, that is, an attempt to permanently order the world of states and markets according to its national interests.

Instead of starting from Washington, the imperial capital, this study of empire lite focuses on how its authority is exercised in three frontier zones – Afghanistan, Bosnia and Kosovo – where a distinctive new form of imperial tutelage called nation-building is taking shape. It is appropriate to call this exercise imperial because, even though the United Nations, independent humanitarian agencies and many other foreign governments are taking part, it was American military power which made nation-building possible in the first place. The alternative account – which is to call nation-building an exercise in 'humanitarian intervention' by a fiction called 'the international community' – actively obscures the fact that none of it would have happened had the United States not decided to use decisive military force. It did so, more-

over, for imperial reasons: to consolidate its global hegemony, to assert and maintain its leadership and to ensure
stability in three zones essential to the security of itself
or its allies.

I am not interested in using the word imperial as an
epithet. I would prefer to use it as a description and to
explore how American imperial power is actually exercised. Nor do I assume that America is all-powerful. Far
from believing that imperial authorities must always be
omnipotent, I want to focus on the limits of American
power and influence. The key question is whether empire
lite is heavy enough to get the job done.

If America is the new Rome, if empire lite is the new
image of empire, there is a more troubling parallel with
antiquity: overwhelming military superiority does not
translate into security. Mastery of the known world does
not confer peace of mind. America has now felt the tremor
of dread that the ancient world must have known when
Rome was first sacked. Then and now an imperial people
has awakened to the menace of the barbarians. Just
beyond the zone of stable democratic states, which took
the World Trade Center and the Pentagon as its headquarters, there are the border zones, like Afghanistan,
where barbarians rule and from where, thanks to modern
technology, they are able to inflict devastating damage on
centres of power far away. Retribution has been visited
on the barbarians, and more will follow, but the American

military knows it has begun a campaign without an obvious end in sight. The most carefree empire in history now grimly confronts the question of whether it can escape Rome's ultimate fate.

At the beginning of the first volume of *The Decline and Fall of the Roman Empire*, published in 1776, Edward Gibbon remarks that empires endure only so long as their rulers take care not to overextend their borders. Augustus bequeathed his successors an empire 'within those limits which nature seemed to have placed as its permanent bulwarks and boundaries: on the west the Atlantic Ocean; the Rhine and Danube on the north; the Euphrates on the east; and towards the south the sandy deserts of Arabia and Africa'. Beyond these boundaries lay the barbarians. But the 'vanity and ignorance' of the Romans, Gibbon went on, led them to 'despise and sometimes to forget the outlying countries which had been left in the enjoyment of a barbarous independence'. As a result, the proud Romans were lulled into making the fatal mistake of 'confounding the Roman monarchy with the globe of the earth'. This characteristic delusion of imperial power, repeated by the British imperialists in their turn, makes the mistake of confusing global power with global hegemony. The Americans may have the former, but they do not have the latter, that is, they cannot reliably control outcomes everywhere, and the more they try the more they expose themselves to the same risks that eventually undermined the classical empires of old.

The war on terror is risky because it appears to require the exercise of American power everywhere at once. Afghanistan is not the only border zone that harbours a barbarian threat. Further pacification operations, covert or overt, beckon in Yemen, Somalia and the Sudan. Al-Qaeda's attempts to launder financial assets have been traced to the Lebanese business circles that control the export of conflict diamonds from Sierra Leone, Liberia, Angola and the Congo. There are likely to be cells to root out in the Philippines and Indonesia. American Special Forces are now deployed to the mountain passes of Georgia to stop infiltration by Chechen guerrillas linked to al-Qaeda. As any Roman legion commander would have known, the more spread out and diffused American military power becomes the more vulnerable each unit is to capture, ambush or hostage-taking.

The empire does not always appear in the new lite form – of Special Forces units and CIA backed by air power. It is also capable of massed formations in the classical mode. An operation against Iraq – requiring more than 250,000 troops – is in prospect, and its goals are imperial: not simply to enforce international law, not merely to control the proliferation of weapons of mass destruction, but to wipe out the leader of Arab rejectionism and go on to reorder the political map of the Middle East on American terms. An American empire that since defeat in Vietnam had been cautious in its designs has been roused by barbarian attack to go on the offensive. There might be reason, even though the awakening has been brutal, to be thankful to the barbarians. After all, they are, as the poet Celan said, a kind of solution. They have offered the empire a new *raison d'être* and a long-term strategic objective: the global eradication of terror.

Such an objective is also a potentially fatal lure. Empires that do not understand the limits of their own capabilities do not survive. Empires that cannot balance pride with prudence do not endure. An endless war on terror tempts the empire to overstretch, and when it over-stretches, it becomes vulnerable.

It is also vulnerable because its enemy is not a state, susceptible to deterrence, influence and coercion, but a shadowy cell of persons who have proved that they cannot be deterred and coerced and who have hijacked a global ideology – Islam – that gives them a bottomless supply of recruits and allies in a global war. They have also hijacked global civil society and exploited its values – mobility and freedom, as well as its technologies – to take war to the heart of the empire. No terrorist campaign can ever succeed unless it can convince large numbers of discontented people that it speaks on behalf of their humiliation. Al Qaeda's terrorists succeeded in making themselves into the representatives of all the resentments of the poor, downtrodden and oppressed in the Islamic world. In the West as well, September 11 was frequently seen as an authentic cry of rage, representing real and sincere resentments. The sincerity and authenticity of this claim to represent the downtrodden may be doubted, but this is of little real comfort. It is true that most forms of terrorism actually impersonate political representation. Terrorists claim to represent causes; in fact, they hijack grievances in order to give violence legitimacy. They try to make violence the first, rather than the last, resort of a politics that seeks redress for injustice and thus to make a peaceful solution impossible.

The terrorists who led the attack of September 11, as an exercise in the politics of the global spectacular, did not even bother to list their grievances. They made no political demands at all, and it seems clear that they were not pursuing properly political goals, so much as seeking to bring down a mighty religious malediction on their adversary. No matter. Into the horrified silence that followed their attack flowed the cheers of the Palestinian and Arab street, who saw in the attacks a revenge for all their humiliations. So long as this identification is as strong as it is, so long as a monstrous cult of martyrdom through violence spreads through the Arab and Muslim worlds, it is cold comfort to insist that terrorists are not sincere and authentic servants of the millions who identify with them. This does not stop millions of people from identifying with their cause. What makes the empire vulnerable is the size and extent of this identification.

Even if they represented nobody but themselves, the attackers of 9/11 were aiming not simply at the United States but at her allies in the Middle East, chiefly Saudi Arabia and Egypt. The US homeland found itself caught in the crossfire of a civil war raging within the Arab world, between America's client regimes and the gathering rage of Islamic revolutionaries who want nothing more than to return the Arab world to AD 640, to the time of the Prophet. It is a civil war between the politics of pure reaction and the politics of the impossible. But it has left the American empire in an exposed position. The attacks of 9/11 laid bare the full extent to which the Arab states, with which the West has been allied since the discovery of oil, had become decayed and incompetent betrayers of their own people. The American empire discovered that, in the Middle East, its local pillars were literally built on sand. It remains to be seen whether a successful operation in Iraq will end up strengthening these pillars or sweeping them away.

But the events of 9/11 laid bare a still deeper fault line. One of the unacknowledged causes of 9/11 has been the coincidence of globalised prosperity in the imperial world with disintegration in the states that achieved independence from the colonial empires of Europe, especially the Arab states. The movements of national liberation that swept through the African and Asian worlds in the 1950s, seeking emancipation from colonial rule, have now run their course and in many cases have failed to deliver on their promise to rule more fairly than the colonial oppressors of the past. The failure to create strong and legitimate state institutions has been particularly obvious in the Arab and Muslim worlds. Collapse of state institutions has been exacerbated by urbanisation, by the remorseless growth of lawless shanty towns that collect populations of unemployed or underemployed males who can see the promise of globalised prosperity in the TVs in every café, but cannot enjoy it themselves. In countries like Pakistan, where the state no longer provides basic services to the poorest, Islamic parties, funded from Saudi Arabia, have stepped into the breach, providing clinics, schools and orphanages where the poor receive both needed services and religious indoctrination.

In these decaying or failing states, America is hated because it is allied with regimes that have failed their people or that repress the national aspirations of the oppressed. In the Middle East, America is damned if it does and damned if it doesn't. It is hated both because it is Israel's mainstay and because even when it supports Palestinian statehood, it gives them no more than a Bantustan. The Palestinian Authority, created by the American-led peace process of the 1990s, was divided by roads and settlements, split into the West Bank and Gaza and incapable of effective self-rule and development.

Even if the Palestinian leadership had been competent and honest, which it was not, it would not have been able to contain the bitterness and frustrations of its own people in such a sham state. Revolt was as inevitable as it was futile. An unjust occupation and illegal settlements by Israel have combined with Palestine's own internal pathologies – corruption, political incompetence, lawlessness and terror – to deny ordinary Palestinians their right to competent and honourable self-rule. Palestine's failure as a political order has turned it into a base for terror and a menace to the state next door.

The story of failed American policy in the Middle East indicates the limits of imperial authority. America may have unrivalled power but it has not been able to build stability wherever it wants on its own terms. Nowhere is this more evident than in the Middle East. Since Roosevelt's embrace of the Saudis and Truman's recognition of Israel, American leadership has driven out other potential arbiters – the Russians and Europeans – while failing to impose its own terms. The Middle East is now halfway through what may prove a hundred years' war, in which two peoples grimly struggle for survival and national self-determination and neither can prevail. There is a solution, but it requires the US to impose a partition and police the border between the two states with its own troops.

If such a solution currently remains out of reach, it is because Americans do not see it as a necessary investment in their own security and because they rightly believe that imperial policing in the Middle East is fraught with peril. Moreover, neither the Israelis nor the Palestinians want an imposed peace. But as both of them unwillingly descend the dark spiral of terror and reprisal, they may find it imposed nonetheless. If this happens, it will confirm an uncomfortable fact about the modern world. Nobody likes empires, but there are some problems for which there are only imperial solutions.

All imperial exercises of power must find a balance between hubris and prudence. The problem that 9/11 lays bare for American power is that terror and technology have collapsed the saving distances that kept America safe from harm. As a result, it is difficult to distinguish between a necessary investment and a catastrophic overreach. The very criteria that determine triage, that enable rulers to choose between the essential and the inessential, have been overturned. Prior to the year 2000, it would have seemed obvious in Washington that a small country like the Yemen was of marginal importance, apart from its function as a refuelling base for American warships. Then came the attack on the USS *Cole*. Then came the discovery that Osama bin Laden's ancestral homeland is in the Yemen.

The Middle East is not the only area of the globe that illustrates the central difficulty of empire, which is to decide which of many demands for the exercise of its power it should actually respond to. Afghanistan's current state is another example of the failure of American imperial strategy to ration effectively the use of force. Afghanistan would never have become a home for al-Qaeda had its institutions not been pulverised by twenty years of civil war, and this in turn would never have happened had the United States not abandoned the country after funding the anti-Soviet Afghan resistance. It created and exploited local proxies to fight an anti-imperial war and then failed to dictate and maintain a peace among the victors. Failing to do so, it found itself, a decade later, confronting the same proxies – Osama bin Laden had been one of the mujahedin receiving American support – now turned into deadly enemies.

But it is not just Afghanistan that illuminates both America's awesome power and her simultaneous vulnerability. When American naval planners looked south from the Suez Canal, they only had bad options. All the potential refuelling stops – Sudan, Somalia, Djibouti, Eritrea and Yemen – are dangerous places for American warships. As the attack on the USS *Cole* made clear, none of the governments in these strategically vital refuelling stops can actually guarantee the safety of their imperial visitors.

America paid too little heed to this. It won the Cold War by virtue of a genuinely strategic act of concentration, but the American imperium post 1991 was consolidated, as the British said of their own empire, in a fit of absence of mind. Successive US administrations after 1991 thought they could have imperial domination on the cheap, ruling the world without putting in place any new imperial architecture – new military alliances, new legal institutions, new international development organisms – for a post-colonial, post-Soviet world to replace those that Roosevelt and Churchill had created for the world after Hitler.

The Greeks taught the Romans to call this failure hubris. It was also a general failure of the historical imagination, an inability to grasp that the emerging crisis of state order in so many overlapping zones of the world would eventually become a security threat at home. One of these danger zones was the Pakistan–Afghan border. During the Cold War, America's imperial interest in the region was confined to preventing the southward march of the Russian bear. The internal stability of Pakistan and its quarrel with India over Kashmir were sideshows. When the Russians retreated, American policy essentially abandoned the region, leaving the Pakistanis to establish control of Afghanistan, through the Taliban. This blunder has forced American policy-makers to realise that this frontier zone, once left to proxies, must now be guided by a disciplined and enduring policy, aimed at rebuilding a stable state in Afghanistan, shoring up Pakistan, without alienating the Indians, and preventing both from a nuclear exchange over Kashmir.

If the barbarian attacks of 9/11 have forced the empire to think strategically and act with imperial resolve, they have also brought home some painful home truths to America's allies. In America's emerging global strategy, its European and Canadian friends have been demoted to reluctant junior partners. This has come as a rude awakening, especially for the Europeans. From the birth of the European Community, Europe believed the myth that economic power could be the equivalent of military might, as well as a compensation for lost imperial grandeur. For fifty years, Europe rebuilt itself economically, while passing on the costs of its defence to the United States. To a degree that would have been unthinkable in 1945, Europe demilitarised itself. Germany, which since Bismarck's defeat of the French at Sedan in 1870 had allied national identity to military prowess, sought in the wake of Hitler's disgrace to free its post-war identity of any militaristic trace, going so far as to make a binding constitutional commitment against foreign use of its troops. A nation like France, whose people had sung the first martial national anthem – 'La Marseillaise' – and had created the first mass conscription army as an expression of republican identity and an instrument of national power, now found itself in the 1990s abandoning military conscription and bringing its defence budget down to less than 2 per cent of its GDP. This was more than just reducing its armed forces and the proportion of national income spent on defence. All European states reduced the martial and military elements in their national identity. In the process of Continental integration, European national identity became post-military and, in this sense, post-national. This opened a widening gap with the United States. It remained, alone among the great powers, a nation in which flag, sacrifice and martial honour remained central to national culture and identity. Even Britain, which thanks to Churchill and victory in 1945, held on to more of the martial components of its identity than any other European state, refocused its identity in the 1980s around a variety of alternative self-images, ranging from multiculturalism to Cool Britannia in the 1990s, all of which were notable for the absence of any reference to the fighting traditions of the country. What nobody grasped was how these changes in European national identity would change the relation with the United States, once the enforced dependency of the Cold War era ended. Europeans who had once invented the very idea of martial pride now looked at American patriotism, the last example of the form, and no longer recognised it as anything but flag-waving extremism. The world's only empire was isolated, not just because it was the biggest power, but also because it was the West's last military nation state. Much of the transatlantic tension of the post-Cold War world related to this transformation. The Europeans thought the Americans were ridiculously militaristic; the Americans thought the

Europeans were defeatist and overly civilised. Throughout the nineties this remained in the harmless realm of invidious cultural comparison. But after 9/11 it became important. Suddenly the consequences of European demilitarisation came home to roost. September 11 rubbed in the lesson that global power is still measured by military capability. The Europeans discovered that they lacked the military instruments to be taken seriously, and that their erstwhile defenders, the Americans, regarded them, in a moment of crisis, with suspicious contempt. Having rallied to the American cause, the NATO liaison officers who arrived at Centcom in Florida had to endure the humiliation of being denied all access to the Command Center where the war against Osama bin Laden was actually being run. The Americans trust their allies so little – the same was true during the Kosovo operation – that they exclude everyone but the British from all but the most menial police work.

Yet the Americans cannot operate a global empire without European diplomatic and economic cooperation. The empire needs legitimacy, and multilateral support is a useful cover. European participation in peacekeeping, nation-building and humanitarian reconstruction is so important that the Americans are required, even when they are unwilling to do so, to include Europeans in the governance of their evolving imperial project. This is why the imperial reconstruction of the Balkans, East Timor,

Afghanistan and elsewhere is a novel departure in the history of empire. In the old imperialism, the empire had a single capital, and its objectives were opposed to those of every other empire. In the new humanitarian empire, power is exercised as a condominium, with Washington in the lead, and London, Paris, Berlin and Tokyo following reluctantly behind.

The humanitarian empire is the new face of an old figure: the democratic free world, the Christian West. It is held together by common elements of rhetoric and self-belief: the idea, if not the practice, of democracy; the idea, if not the practice, of human rights; the idea, if not the practice, of equality before the law. Yet the fissures in this imperial project are not just between rhetoric and reality. There is also a deeper contradiction between empire itself and democracy. America itself is a product of an eighteenth-century revolt against empire; all of the states reluctantly linked to the American imperial project are ex-imperial powers consciously attempting to put their imperial ways behind them. Yet here they are, in the new millennium, yoked to a superpower, enforcing, with good or ill grace, the new rules of empire on the barbarians. The contradictions are not happy, but they are unchangeable. Since 1945, each European state has had to make the same difficult transition, from the possession of empire and full Westphalian statehood to pooling sovereignty with other European states and then hitching their stars to the might of the United States. They have each done so because pooling sovereignty with neighbours is more efficient and effective than struggling to maintain sovereignty alone. Hitching their destiny to the United States is not attractive, but it is better than being marginalised.

The Americans essentially dictate Europe's place in this new grand design. US policy choices are unsentimental. It is multilateral when it wants to be, unilateral when it must, and it uses its power to enforce a new international division of labour in which America does the fighting, the Canadians, French, British and Germans do the police patrols in the border zones and the Dutch, Swiss and Scandinavians provide the humanitarian aid.

This is a very different picture of the world than the one entertained by liberal international lawyers and human rights activists who had hoped to see American power integrated into a transnational legal and economic order, organised around the United Nations, the World Trade Organisation, the International Criminal Court and international human rights organisms. A new international order is emerging, but it is crafted to suit American imperial objectives. It is not crafted to tie Gulliver down with a thousand legal strings. The empire signs on to those pieces of the transnational legal order that suit its purposes (the WTO, for example), while ignoring or even sabotaging those parts (the International Criminal Court or the Kyoto protocol) that do not.

Introduction

A new form of ostensibly humanitarian empire – in which Western powers, led by the United States, band together to rebuild state order and reconstruct war-torn societies for the sake of global stability and security – presents humanitarian agencies with the dilemma of how to keep humanitarian programmes from being suborned to imperial interests. These agencies – UNICEF, UNHCR, the International Committee of the Red Cross, – are dependent on Western governments for their funding, yet they struggle to keep a space free to meet humanitarian need irrespective of the political wishes of their paymasters. Yet humanitarian relief cannot be kept distinct from imperial projects, not least because humanitarian action is only possible, in many instances, if imperial armies have first cleared the ground and made it safe for humanitarians to act. It was American air power that made peace and humanitarian reconstruction possible, first in Bosnia, then in Kosovo, and finally in Afghanistan. Humanitarians know that there are some humanitarian problems for which there are only imperial solutions. This forces them to be, like the European states, unwilling and unhappy accomplices of the imperial project.

While the Europeans are resentful accomplices of an international order designed and policed by the Americans, the case is different with the Chinese and the Russians. In the short term, until Russian resource revenues rebuild the Russian state, Vladimir Putin has no choice but to ally with the imperial war on terror, and the Chinese too have signed up, since they want help with their Islamic separatists. But in the longer term, the American bases in Afghanistan, Tajikistan and Uzbekistan are bound to strike the Chinese and the Russians as a challenge, and when the opportunity presents itself, they will respond accordingly. Given the challenge that American power presents to the interests of these states, there is no reason to suppose that American hegemony will result, long-term, in an acquiescent or quiescent global order.

This is an introductory sketch of the new world of geopolitics we live in. The essays in this book focus in detail on only one part of the new world of empire. They attempt to understand the phenomenon of state collapse and state failure in the world's danger zones and the Western response. I focus on nation-building in Bosnia, Kosovo and Afghanistan because they are laboratories in which a new imperium is taking shape, in which American military power, European money and humanitarian motive have combined to produce a form of imperial rule for a post-imperial age. If this sounds contradictory, it is because the impulses that have gone into this new exercise of power are contradictory. On the one hand, the semi-official ideology of the Western world – human rights – sustains the principle of self-determination, the right of

20

each people to rule themselves free of outside interference. This was the ethical principle that, together with defeat and exhaustion by the imperial powers themselves, inspired the decolonisation of Asia and Africa after World War II. Now we are living through the collapse into disorder of many of these former colonial states. Into the resulting vacuum of chaos and massacre a new imperialism has reluctantly stepped, reluctantly because these places are dangerous and because they seemed, at least until 9/11, to be marginal to the interests of the powers concerned. But gradually this reluctance has been replaced by a concerted understanding of why order needs to be brought to these places. Nowhere, after all, could have been more distant than Afghanistan, yet it was in this remote and desperate place that the attacks of 9/11 were prepared. Terror has collapsed distance, and with this collapse has come a sharpened focus in imperial capitals on the necessity of bringing order to the barbarian zones. Bringing order is the paradigmatic imperial task, but it is essential, both for reasons of economy and for reasons of principle, to do so without denying local peoples their rights to some degree of self-determination. The old imperialism, at least in the twentieth century, justified itself as a mission to civilise, to prepare tribes and lesser breeds in the habits of self-discipline necessary for the exercise of self-rule. Self-rule did not necessarily have to happen soon – the imperial administrators hoped to enjoy the imperial sunset as long as possible – but it was held out as a distant incentive, and the incentive was crucial in co-opting local elites and preventing them from passing into open rebellion. In the new imperialism, this promise of self-rule cannot be kept so distant, for local elites are all creations of modern nationalism, and modern nationalism's primary ethical content is the imperative of self-determination. Local elites, accordingly, must be 'empowered' to take over as soon as the American imperial forces have restored order and the European humanitarians have rebuilt the roads, schools and houses. Nation-building seeks to reconcile imperial power and local self-determination through the medium of an exit strategy. This is imperialism in a hurry: to spend money, to get results, to turn the place back to the locals and get out. But it is similar to the old imperialism in the sense that real power in these zones – Kosovo, Bosnia and Afghanistan – remains in imperial capitals. Local satraps, even if elected by their own people, exercise limited power, even if in name their states are sovereign. The new imperialism is creating a new form of sub-sovereignty, in which states exercise independence in name, without real independence in fact, as formal or informal protectorates of the great powers. The ostensible motive that sustains these nation-building projects may be humanitarian, but the real principle is imperial: the maintenance of order over barbarian threat.

Introduction

These essays are not intended as an exercise in irony or cynicism. Humanitarian action is not unmasked if it is shown to be the instrument of imperial power. Motives are not discredited just because they are shown to be mixed. It is entirely unsurprising that America and Europe invest in these zones of danger for motives that include just as much callow self-interest as high humanitarian resolve. Nor is the exercise of imperial power discreditable in itself, provided that empire does more than reproduce itself, provided that it does eventuate in self-rule for nations and peoples. Those who pick up this book expecting a denunciation of American imperialism, or imperialism in general, will be disappointed. An empire that created stable, democratic institutions and the rule of law in Bosnia, Kosovo and Afghanistan and then left would be doing something creditable, useful to American and European interests to be sure, but also useful to the local population. An empire that invaded and then exited in easy disgust at the obduracy of the problems and the sullen resistance of the local population would be less admirable. An imperial invasion of Iraq that replaced a hostile tyrant with a friendly one would be unworthy of support. At the moment, these imperial exercises hang in the balance: no one actually knows whether they will work, whether Afghanistan, Kosovo, Bosnia and now Iraq will ever achieve sustained democratic self-government. That is the test, and critics of imperial methods need to understand that self-government in these places is unattainable without some exercise of imperial power. The central paradox, true of Japan and Germany in 1945, and true today, is that imperialism has become a precondition for democracy. The Iraqi opposition will never overcome tyranny without an American and British military victory, followed by a long occupation. The Afghan people will never overcome the rule of the warlords and consolidate their own form of peaceful self-rule without a preliminary military occupation by foreign powers. To be sure, the only form of empire that is compatible with democracy is temporary empire, but it is empire nonetheless.

What help local people need from their temporary imperial rulers should be up to them. They should be the ones who decide what kinds of democracy, rule of law and stability of property can be successfully absorbed in their culture and context. There is nothing odious or invidious about helping local people find their way to the right institutional mixture, provided that they have a say in their own institutional design. The problem with the new imperialism, as these pages hope to show, is not that it is imperial, i.e. it uses force and power to reorder the world. The problem is that those who believe in the use of imperial means do not practise what they preach. We say we believe in self-determination, and we confiscate all power into our own hands; we say we respect local cultures and traditions, and yet we are often as contemptuous, behind the locals' backs, as the imperialists of old. Finally, we say we are going to stay the course, when we are always looking for the exit. Nation-building could be an exercise in solidarity between rich and poor, the possessors and the dispossessed. Too often, it is an exercise in mutual betrayal. From betrayal comes resentment and from resentment comes rebellion. There is no necessary reason, certainly nothing in its humanitarian rhetoric, to save the new imperialism from the failure and discredit that befell the old. Yet failure, while it would rejoice the enemies of the West, would ultimately do the poor and oppressed no good at all. The purpose of these essays is to help both sides in the enterprise of nation-building, to identify the illusions that make a genuine act of solidarity so difficult, and finally to suggest what needs to be done so that people can actually reclaim the right to rule themselves.

The Bridge Builder

In 1566, when the Ottoman Empire was at its height, and its sway extended from Constantinople to Budapest, an Ottoman engineer, named Hayreddin, came to the city of Mostar, in south-western Bosnia, to build a bridge across the River Neretva. All we know about him was that he was a pupil of Sinan, architect-in-chief to Suleiman the Magnificent. Engineers like Hayreddin built the bath-houses in Budapest, mosques in Sarajevo and bridges over the rivers in the empire, all in plain white, long-enduring stone. The bridge he built over the Neretva had a polit-ical purpose: to mark the boundary between Ottoman possessions and the hinterland of Ragusa, a wealthy city state on the Adriatic coast, now known as Dubrovnik. The Ottomans had reached Mostar in 1467 and they had torn down the Ragusan Bridge. Now in 1566, they were ready to put up their own.

Hayreddin seems to have worked with a small team of local stonemasons, together with a craftsman or two from Constantinople. They quarried the stone from the austere cliffs above the town, and dragged it down to the river bank on sleds pulled by draught animals. They cut it into shape with saws and poured molten lead into seams cut into the blocks to hold the bridge span together, and they seem to have made their share of mistakes. It is not easy to anticipate, for example, whether the wooden scaffolding on which the stone is laid will actually bear the weight. They almost certainly lost more than a few pieces of stone into the blue and green waters of the Neretva.

Bridges are functional structures: this one's function was to symbolise imperial authority and to connect the mosques and markets of one side of the city to the other. Yet for reasons we will never understand, Hayreddin's artisans turned their bridge into a work of exceptional beauty. It's unlikely that this beauty was understood from the beginning. It takes time for bridges to work their way into people's affections and still longer to become part of the identity of a town. All we know is that when the Ottomans were driven out of Bosnia in the 1890s, the bridge was not torn down, even though it no longer had much of a function, not being wide enough for big loads, and certainly not for the automobiles that began to penetrate this remote part of southern Europe. The bridge endured through the First World War, when the Serbs and Austro-Hungarians fought in the region and it survived the Second World War, through all the furious partisan combat that convulsed Bosnia. In Tito's Yugoslavia, the bridge became famous, and by the 1960s and 1970s tour buses would bring people from all over southern Europe to see it.

I saw the old bridge once myself. In 1959, my father and mother and brother and I drove from Belgrade to Dubrovnik, through Sarajevo and Mostar, in a heavy black Buick. We stopped in Sarajevo and went into the big mosque in the middle of the old town bazaar. It was the first time I had ever been in a mosque, the first time it dawned on me that there were European Muslims and that they had been here for centuries. We knelt in one corner and watched how they took off their shoes in the archway at the entrance, put on little slippers, washed their hands in the fountain and then went inside to kneel and touch their foreheads and palms on the expanse of carpet in the cool domed space inside.

My diary of the trip is full of twelve-year-old thoughts, but it is clear even then how much the old bridge over the Neretva impressed me. It was made of a beautifully aged white stone, and it soared over the rushing blue water below, and it seemed impossibly delicate, too thin to take the weight of a horse or a man. But it bore all the weights put upon it, and we crossed to and fro, visiting the mosques and bazaar stalls that clustered on the Muslim side – and the Roman Catholic churches, Viennese-style pastry shops and municipal offices on the Croatian side.

Calling them Muslim and Croat sides of the river isn't really correct. While the two populations did live separately, Croats and Muslims were to be found on both sides of the Neretva, and the 120,000 citizens of Mostar did think of themselves as two peoples sharing a city and a bridge.

It is well known that in 1992–3 madness descended upon the townspeople of Mostar. At least, madness is how they talk about it now. At the time, of course, it all seemed, if not sane, then at least necessary to divide into two warring camps, to defend yourself and to drive your neighbours across the river. The madness went on for eighteen months. Muslim and Croat militias composed of young men who often had been in the same class at school rained fire on each other, at first across the river, then street by street and finally house by house. Ten years later, you can still see how crazy it was, from the way the buildings have been taken apart, not in big chunks by artillery or mortars, but chipped apart, bullet by bullet, by small arms fire at point-blank range. By the time it was over, the city was divided in two: Muslims driven out of the Croat side, Croats driven out of the Muslim side and nothing but gunfire across the river between them.

During this time, a particular act of madness occurred that people still find painful to talk about. On 9 November 1993, an artillery unit from the Croatian side of the city, which had been firing for two days, managed to bring down the old bridge. An amateur cameraman recorded the scene. On the footage, you see a puff of cordite and the soaring vault drops, like a dead beast, into the river.

You could put the destruction of the bridge down to the mad vandalism of war, but that still leaves you with some explaining to do. In a city like Mostar, given its identity by the bridges – there are actually six of them – destroying the oldest of them was a perverse act of self-mutilation. The bridge, after all, was built into the very meaning of the town. The word Mostar means 'bridge-keeper'.

Everybody knows who did it, by the way. The artillery commander still lives in Mostar, on the Croatian side.

The Croatian vice-mayor of the city, Mr Tomić, admits that his people destroyed the bridge. 'This is a fact that cannot be denied,' he says, which considering the number of facts commonly denied in Bosnia on all sides says something for his candour. Then he adds a remark that lights up the psychology of post-war denial. 'For a long time afterwards the Croats said, "it was their bridge, so what do we care?"'

Mr Tomić smiles ruefully at his fellow Croats. 'Now they are beginning to realise. Yes, it is our bridge too.'

In 'Heart of Darkness', Joseph Conrad remarked that empire, when observed close-up, is not a pretty sight. What redeems it, he said, is only the idea. The reconstruction of the Balkans has not been an exercise in humanitarian social work. It has always been an imperial project, driven by a clear, if reluctantly grasped imperative to replace the collapsed Communist imperium of Tito's era with a new architecture of states that would bring stability to a combustible corner of Europe. Why else would there be 12,000 troops in Bosnia and thousands more in Kosovo under the command of American generals, together with experts from many nations investing billions in an otherwise marginal part of the continent? The aim is to integrate the Balkan peninsula – eventually – into the architecture of Europe, and, in the meantime, to reduce the flow of its major exports: crime, refugees and drugs.

Yet this is not all that is at stake. Nation-building would lack all soulfulness if it were just about creating stability in zones important to Western interests. The idea that redeems nation-building is the spiritual component, assisting former enemies to reconcile, to bind up their wounds and transcend a painful past. This is what gives the imperial project its moral allure.

In Mostar, the locals took some time to realise that what the internationals wanted for their investment was a show of reconciliation. Even after a ceasefire concluded in 1994, the hatred on both sides remained intense and visceral. Military-aged men, above the age of seventeen, were banned from crossing to the other side. In January 1996, a Muslim boy defied the ban and drove across to see a Croatian girl who had been a neighbour of his before his family was driven out. The boy was shot in the back of the head by the Croatian police and died, slumped over the wheel of his car as he crossed the bridge back on to the Muslim side.

It took ten years before Croats agreed with Muslims: it was time to rebuild the old bridge. This change of heart may have had to do with both sides realising that the division of the city into two was costing them money. In Mostar, there is two of everything: bus companies, hospitals, garbage collection companies, even universities (so-called). Duplication is bankrupting the city. Besides, the internationals that foot the bills are tired of the Mostar impasse and want to go home. So let's not speak of some grand new spirit of reconciliation. Let's just suppose that people are getting practical.

Naturally, the man they have found to lead the team to rebuild the old bridge is neither Croat nor Muslim. He is a middle-aged French *ingénieur des ponts et chaussées*, Gilles Pequeux. He is a rumpled and modest figure, with a melancholy air, who has an office in an old two-storey stone house about fifty yards from where the old bridge stood. It is a neat office, with a bare white table, and the walls are decorated with old lithographs, photos and drawings of the bridge as it used to be, together with pieces of Ottoman ironwork salvaged from the river.

Mr Pequeux has lived in Mostar on and off since January 1995. When he first arrived, the Muslims and Serbs were still fighting in the rest of Bosnia, while in the city itself, the European Union was trying to reinforce a precarious peace signed between the Muslims and the Croats. The town had a European Union mayor whose job it was to get both sides of the river to work together. The six bridges across the Neretva were down and it was Pequeux's job to rebuild them.

He was told that it was impossible to hire crews from both sides of the river, but he went ahead anyway, and Croat and Muslim workmen struggled together in the cold water of the Neretva, building the caissons and sinking the pilings necessary to hold up the supports for the bridges that began to rise and reconnect both sides of the town. Bridge-building, as Pequeux sees it, doesn't have to wait for hatreds to cool. He just built the bridges and waited for people to use them. At first, nobody did. The Croats would sit in the cafés on one side, and the Muslims would sit in cafés on the other. You could be in big trouble if you fraternised. But now, six years later, there is a lot of traffic across the bridges, and shoals of teenagers eddy to and fro, at least until darkness falls.

The fact that Pequeux is French happens to be impor-tant. For French kings and emperors, engineers were just as important as they were to the Sultans of Constantinople. Louis XIV, for example, had a great engineer, Vauban, who built forts and bridges throughout France. Napoleon founded the École des Ponts et Chaussées so that he could lay French roads and bridges along the expanse of his empire. Pequeux trained at Napoleon's *École* and bridges rouse him to brief flights of passion. They are, he says, '*une alliance magique de savoir-faire*', a magical alliance of different crafts: architecture, engineering, masonry and carpentry.

He has watched, with bemusement, the way a bridge nobody wanted to talk about is now suddenly a subject on everybody's lips. A few years ago, the Turkish president flew into Mostar and promised Turkish money to rebuild the bridge. It was, he said, a symbol of the Ottoman, Muslim and Turkish influence in Europe. He did not need to add that the Turkish government is campaigning for entry to the European Union. The problem for the Turks is that the Europeans don't exactly remember Ottoman rule as a golden age. In the Balkans, people often call it the Turkish yoke, and even the Western Europeans, who were never ruled by the Turks, have their own reasons to resist the Turkish claim to rebuild the bridge. The Germans especially don't want Turkey in the European club, since it would mean even more Turkish immigration. So the Europeans decided that they would pay for the bridge. The French government supports Pequeux's team. There is some irony in the fact that Europeans want both to keep the Turks out and to rebuild the bridge as a symbol of its multicultural and Muslim heritage.

Six billion dollars was committed to Bosnian reconstruction after Dayton. But the link between physical and mental reconstruction, between rebuilding infrastructure and reconciling mentalities remains unclear. The roads, bridges and schools are rebuilt and the power lines are working again. Red-tiled roofs are back on most houses, but inside the minds of the inhabitants, there remain fears, memories and hatreds still too deep for healing. In the six years of peace, these emotions have mostly produced political paralysis. Bosnia is divided into three entities: Republika Srpska, a sickle-shaped belt of land, bordering Serbia and reaching right to the outskirts of Sarajevo; a federation for the Croats and the Muslims; and a third level of government – the national institutions of Bosnia–Herzegovina. No small country has more levels of government, more politicians, and more possibilities for corruption, extortion or impasse. A couple of years ago, the Bosnian parliament spent a week debating whether the front page of the passport that all Bosnia-Herzegovinans carry should list the ethnic entity they come from, and if so, how high the lettering for that line should be. In the end, the High Representative, an international official who functions as a kind of viceroy, had to step in and decide because the three sides were deadlocked.

On a recent trip back to Bosnia, my first since 1996, I went to a party at the UN headquarters in Sarajevo for a general of the French gendarmerie, who was going home after running the UN operation to train a new Bosnian police and to weed out the bad cops. This general, a short prickly character, had fired more bad cops in a single year than all his predecessors. I told him that I had come to Bosnia to study nation-building. Nation-building? He looked me up and down with a mixture of pity and scorn: '*Mes condoléances, Monsieur.*'

Bosnia after Dayton offered laboratory conditions in which to experiment with nation-building. Now the money is almost spent, and Western governments are heading for the exits. The UN mission to train the police will be finishing up at the end of this year. 'We are declaring victory and going home,' one UN official told me sardonically. International disillusionment is palpable. Instead of flowing towards reconstruction, much of the international money has ended up in the wrong pockets. The Jaguars, Audis and BMWs parked outside the Serbian government building in Banja Luka would do a New York nightclub parking lot proud. Throughout Bosnia, rule of law is next to non-existent, because there are still no independent prosecutors, judges or lawyers. Mostar is still ruled by people who rose to power during the years of war and madness.

Leaders from both communities meet only for photo

opportunities with visiting foreign dignitaries. Otherwise, they do not fraternise. Yet they have learned that funds for Mostar will dry up unless displays of multi-ethnic cooperation are forthcoming. What better display could there be of Mostar turning over a new leaf than for politicians from both sides to pose together on a reconstructed bridge?

So reconstruction has not even commenced, and yet the project is already carrying some heavy symbolic loads. It has become a metaphor, a bridge from the past to the future, a bridge between Croats and Muslims, a bridge between the internationals and the locals, and a bridge between the Muslim world and Europe. The problem with all this metaphorical weight is that the promised reconciliation hasn't actually occurred. Yes, people cross from one side to the other. But they still live completely separate lives. So, instead of symbolising reconciliation, the restored bridge will be there to provide a substitute.

When traumatised peoples fail to play out our script of reconciliation, we tend to blame them, rather than our own wishful thinking. In fact, while it is no less divided than, say, Belfast, Bosnia is also no more divided. You can emphasise the sullen faces of the men in the cafés of the Serbian enclave of Foca, as they watch the international patrols pass their door. One look at their eyes makes the Western fantasy of reconciliation seem ridiculous. Alternatively, you could draw hope from the Muslim refugees who have returned to Srebrenica, to Prijedor, places that were once synonyms for hatred and murder. These refugee returns, half-returns really, since the families keep some of their members safely in Germany, could be taken either as proof that rebuilding multi-ethnicity is difficult, or as a sign that it is happening despite everything.

Bosnians, of all ethnic groups, would be shallow creatures indeed if they did not hold on to memory and pain. Yet we are impatient with their memory, impatient with their reluctance to be reconciled. We are in a hurry. We are leaving, in part, because they have failed to provide us with the requisite happy ending.

The rebuilding of the Mostar Bridge is one last chance for a happy ending, a metaphor as important to the internationals as it is to the locals. The result of all this metaphor mongering, as the French engineer realises, is that everybody wants the bridge rebuilt by tomorrow morning. And it is here that Pequeux has dug his heels in. He says it may take a year yet. His studies are not finished. He hasn't trained his craftsmen. Nobody can understand these delays, but from where he sits, in the old Ottoman house a stone's throw from the forlorn stumps of the bridge, it seems that everybody – the Turks, the Europeans, the locals – is more interested in the bridge as bearer of their loads of illusion than they are in actually rebuilding it properly.

He would not say so himself, but the cost of caring more for symbols than for reality is on display nearby. Another team is rebuilding Criva Cuprija, a little bridge over a tributary that runs into the Neretva. The team already has the forest of wooden scaffolding up, and stone by stone the new span is being put into place. A big sign announces that the Duchy of Luxembourg is paying for the project. It is a Disney-like version of what an old bridge should look like. For example, instead of bonding the stones together with invisible seams of liquid lead, poured into runnels carved into the stone, the Luxembourg bridge-builders are bonding the stones with cement used in Luxembourg. This is the kind of short cut that the desire for easy metaphors of reconciliation can lead you to take.

If you want the real thing, it takes time, says Pequeux. You have to study what Hayreddin had in mind. You have to find the old plans in Ottoman archives in Istanbul; you can't just work from photographs. You have to establish where the original stone came from. You have to figure out how it was cut, and how they used molten lead to bond the ironwork that held the stones in place. Pequeux takes you down to the Neretva gorge, and you stand below where the bridge used to be, and there are pieces of the old bridge littered about, and he can tell you where each piece used to fit, how it was cut, and point out the mason's marks. This Frenchman's devoted attention to the bridge is a kind of love, notable because – and this comes as a shock – Pequeux had never actually seen it. By the time he reached Mostar in 1995, the bridge had been lying in pieces in the river for two years. So when I told him that I had seen it as a child, a fleeting look of longing crossed his face.

There is also growing respect for Hayreddin and his fellow bridge-builders, four centuries back. Pequeux has discovered that two completely different ways of cutting stone – one European, the other Ottoman – were used on the bridge. The cutters from Constantinople, to judge from etchings of the time and from the marks of their saws in the stone, cut straight on, while the Europeans approached the stone sideways. No one knows why these two civilisations did a common task so differently, but both civilisations mark the stones of the bridge.

Pequeux decided that the only way to do the job properly was to persuade the French government to finance a school of stonecutters in Mostar to teach a new generation these two old ways of cutting stone. French stonemasons are currently training Croats and Muslims to work stone in the old way in a building on the Croatian side. When the bridge goes up, they will do it the way Hayreddin did. Pequeux wants them to understand that the beauty of the original lay in its imperfections, in the misjudgements, in the millimetres of missed connections between the stones that vaulted the twenty-nine metres from one side to the other. Beauty – the engineer says – is built from mistakes.

So, I say, gesturing at all the loose stone gathered on the river bank below the bridge, you are going to put these back up exactly where they were? Pequeux looks disappointed. I have clearly understood nothing at all. 'We are not going to use the old stones. It's not going to be the old bridge. It's going to be a new bridge.'

'A new old bridge,' I venture.

Exactly like the old bridge, yes, but a new one. '*Un nouveau vieux pont.*'

He walks me back to my hotel through the Croatian part of Mostar, past the front-line areas where the small arms fighting was so intense – house to house, wall to wall even – that no one could tell who was shooting whom. On one pockmarked wall there is a spray-painted sentence that reads: How do you sleep?

Our sleep is unlikely to be disturbed by what happened in Mostar, then or now. The Western need for noble victims and happy endings suggests that we are more interested in ourselves than we are in the places, like Bosnia, that we take up as causes. This may be the imperial kernel at the heart of the humanitarian enterprise. For what is empire but the desire to imprint our values, civilisation and achievements on the souls, bodies and institutions of another people? Imperialism is a narcissistic enterprise, and narcissism is doomed to disillusion.

Whatever other people want to be, they do not want to be forced to be us. It is an imperial mistake to suppose that we can change their hearts and minds. It is their memory, their trauma, not ours, and intervention is not therapy. We can help them to rebuild the bridge. Whether they actually use it to heal a city is up to them.

The bridge project will cost about ten million dollars, and when it is finished, maybe next year, maybe later, big shots will come and have their pictures taken, and the tour buses will resume, and the trinket sellers will have a market, and Mostar will proclaim itself reunited. But the man who has made it possible, the *ingénieur des ponts et chaussées*, is not so sure that his bridge will bear the symbolic weight it will be asked to carry. It will be a *nouveau vieux pont*, because there is really no way back to the bridge that Hayreddin built, just as there is no way back to the way Mostar was before the madness came. The bridge project, the engineer realises, raises one of the central questions about nation- building. How do you build bridges between people? How do you help people to heal? Can outsiders actually do much at all? And what about the power of beauty? The hardest part about the Mostar story is that the beauty of the bridge did not save it from madness. We do want to believe that beauty can help people resist the call of death and division. Only time will tell if beauty will be given a second chance.

The Humanitarian
as Imperialist

Bernard Kouchner is wearing a lime-green open-necked
shirt, sports jacket, slacks and dark glasses. He's walking
along a dusty road between wheat fields in Kosovo with
a Spanish general and two Kosovar politicians, while a TV
crew retreats slowly backwards, recording their advance.
It is a bright July day in the year 2000. Although it has
been thirteen months since NATO called off its bombing
campaign and the Serbian Army trooped out of Kosovo,
soldiers keep telling the camera crew to stick to the path:
the gentle wheat fields may be mined.

At the place where the dirt road crosses a railway track,
a team of soldiers, some of them wearing latex gloves, is
bent over, combing between the railway ties; others are
measuring distances with tape; still others are taking
pictures.

Just across the tracks, wrenched sideways, are the fire-
scorched remains of a rusty red van. Where the engine

used to be, there is a hole; where the driver's seat used to be is another hole; and where the driver's door used to be is a twisted flange of metal. Tumbled about on the ground are crates of bottled beer that have spilled from the side door of the van.

Bernard Kouchner, special representative of the United Nations Secretary-General in Kosovo, removes his dark glasses and stops in front of the wreckage. His job is to rebuild Kosovo and to get the Kosovar majority to live side by side with the remaining Serb minority. The charred and twisted van is yet another proof that this objective still remains out of reach. A British brigadier, who must have seen this kind of incident a few times in Northern Ireland, scans the computer printout from his battalion incident room and reports that his patrol heard the explosion at 10.50 a.m.

'But I was told the mine was planted at five in the morning,' Kouchner says.

'Most likely, sir,' the brigadier replies. 'Professional job. Not an amateur drive-by. It would have taken someone ten to fifteen minutes to dig the mine. No wires or timer. A pressure detonation.'

When the British patrol reached the scene, there was nothing left of Zlatko Delić or Bojan Filipović, two Serbs who had been in the beer delivery van. Bojan's brother Borko, who was also in the van, was still alive, though one of his legs had been blown off and what remained of the other might have to be amputated.

And who was responsible? The British brigadier couldn't possibly speculate. Kosovo is crawling with undercover intelligence agents from a dozen countries, but they report to their national capitals, not to the local NATO commanders. The one certainty is that the dirt track linked two Serb villages. It seems obvious that Kosovar Albanians have sneaked through the fields in the dead of night and planted a mine at exactly the spot they could expect Serbs – any Serbs – to slow down and change gear to get over the railway tracks.

The photographers are now in position. The TV cameras are rolling. Kouchner puts his arms firmly behind the backs of Ibrahim Rugova and Hashim Thaci, the two leading Kosovar Albanian politicians, and nudges them forward so that they can all be photographed looking at what is presented – without a word being said – as another Kosovar Albanian attack on Serbs. This is the first time Thaci and Rugova, inveterate enemies and rivals for power, have appeared together to denounce what Kouchner calls 'a terrorist attack upon the peace process'.

It is widely believed that Thaci, also known as 'the snake' when he was a guerrilla commander of the Kosovo Liberation Army, may know more about who is behind this and other similar attacks than he lets on. Most Serbs believe his ex-KLA men are in fact responsible. Thaci knows what Kouchner expects of him, so he runs through

47

his lines with a solemn face, condemning, regretting, affirming and so on.

Rugova, looking ill and shrunken, stares glumly down at the dirt, and when it is his turn, only mumbles: 'We need to work in order not to have another tragic occasion. We need to change opinions in Kosovo.' The speeches are meagre and perfunctory, but Kouchner pronounces himself satisfied. 'The fascists must not prevail,' he says, in his Maurice Chevalier English. When he was France's minister of state for humanitarian action in the 1980s, the media used to call Kouchner 'the minister of indignation'. In this bare field in the south Balkans, his indignation sounds as if it has all been said too often.

As soon as the show is over, Kouchner works his way through the small group of journalists, with an arm around the shoulder for one, a quiet word for another. Thaci, too, briefly strokes the local press before jumping into his car and racing off through the howls of furious men lining the roads of the nearby Serbian village. As Kouchner passes these crowds, behind the tinted windows of his armoured jeep, the Serb men look at him in angry silence. 'You've heard of virtual war,' one member of his staff whispers, wearily. 'Well, that was virtual peacemaking.'

Getting Thaci and Rugova to the scene of the crime is supposed to isolate the terrorists, to demonstrate that violence does not represent the will of the Kosovar people. Yet there is a conspiracy of silence in support of these acts among ordinary Kosovars, and the politicians' condemnations in front of the cameras seem less convincing as a political message than the dirty red van with its guts ripped apart.

In the walled precinct of the Serb monastery at Gračanica, where Kouchner's convoy appears next, the only person there to greet them is the bishop's 'chief of protocol', an apologetic Serbian woman in her twenties, who says that the bishop is away but that his deputy, the Revd Sava Janjić, is on his way. Kouchner whiles away the time in a high-timbered refectory, decorated with pictures of all the Serbian churches dynamited or rocketed by the Kosovars since the 'liberation' of the province in June 1999. Today, the minarets of the Kosovar mosques are being rebuilt, brick by brick, while Orthodox churches remain in ruins.

In repose, Kouchner is different from Kouchner on show: he looks deflated, wanders to and fro, cadges a cigarette from an aide, frets a pair of black worry beads between his fingers. Will virtual peacemaking of this sort work? 'Not by itself,' he says with that Gallic shrug the French have perfected for moments when they are forced to admit a fact but don't want to take responsibility for it.

Father Sava, a bespectacled monk with the distracted air of a bright but harried graduate student, rushes in, sweating from climbing the flight of stairs. He beckons Kouchner and the Spanish general to be seated. A spare chair is kept empty between the two of them for Bishop Artemije, Father Sava's superior.

The two men are the leaders of the 'monastery moderates', the UN's wishful phrase for the Gračanica Serbs. Moderation in Kosovo is a complicated thing. Wherever there is a peacekeeping operation, in the zones of ethnic war, a diligent search is always made for 'moderates', that is, a local leadership who can be made to do the bidding of the international interveners. Their dilemma as local leaders is that the more pliable they are to the will of internationals, the less credibility they have with their local population, and the less use they ultimately prove to be to the internationals. The international community does not want to rule through puppets, since puppets will never last. The trouble is that puppets are usually all they can find. In the case of Father Sava, moderation simply means that he has been willing to talk to Kouchner and even take part in meetings with Kosovar Albanians. But Father Sava represents only a minority of Serbs. Most of them live in the enclave of Mitrovica, and their leadership won't have any part of Kouchner's attempts to create dialogue between the two sides. Kouchner tells the monk that he has come to express his condolences at the latest attack. The Spanish general chimes in with a promise in his broken English 'to increase the tempo of our operations'.

None of this means much to Father Sava. Only a week before, NATO patrols had failed to stop a grenade attack in a Gračanica market. And the attacks on Serb churches continue despite NATO's efforts. Kouchner tries to soothe the monk's nerves with promises of continuing political support.

'We are trying to endure the pressures,' Father Sava replies, looking bleak and uneasy. The pressures are not just from Kosovar hit squads with grenades; they also come from Serbian hotheads outside the monastery walls who don't think the father should be talking to Kouchner at all. 'I can only say where it hurts,' Father Sava says plaintively to Kouchner. 'You will have to find the cure. You're the doctor.'

He is a doctor, an MD, and in this case, his patient is a rugged, south Balkan province the size of Connecticut that remains on life support a year after the NATO intervention. Getting Kosovo to stand on its own feet again – in truth, building its entire political and economic infrastructure from nothing – is the most ambitious project the UN has ever undertaken. Kouchner and a staff of several thousand have restarted the schools, found shelter for hundreds of thousands of returning refugees and established an official currency – the German mark. Their signal failure, so far, has been to get Kosovars to live with the remaining Serbs. This is a significant embarrassment: the NATO intervention was defended as a human rights

51

operation, to put a stop to Slobodan Milošević's ethnic cleansing. It stopped Milošević, but it has not stopped the Kosovars attempting to drive out the remaining Serbs. A cloud of disillusion has descended over the Kosovo operation, and by extension to all such exercises in humanitarian intervention. What is the point of assisting people to be free if they use their freedom to persecute their former persecutors? The moral script that justifies humanitarian intervention demands noble victims and the Kosovars are not playing by the script. This kind of hatred gives Kouchner a huge political problem: donors won't pony up the money for rebuilding, and countries won't send contingents of soldiers and police because they don't want to be seen aiding a nasty new ethnic majority tyranny in Kosovo. As Veton Surroi, the sardonic publisher of Kosovo's best daily, *Koha Ditore*, puts it, 'Morality was your investment here, so you expect morality as your payback.' But instead of moral payback, there is just revenge killing.

Kouchner is not just another European politician making a second career in the Balkans. He is perhaps the key figure in the strange mutation of modern humanitarian action. Thirty years ago, he started out as a young doctor working for the International Red Cross during the civil war between the Biafran secessionists and the Nigerian government. The Red Cross, then, and now, practised the rule of silent neutrality, never publicly commenting on the crimes or abuses its delegates witnessed as they handed out relief. This was the code of silence, for example, which led the Red Cross not to disclose what it had seen at Auschwitz. There, its delegates visited Allied prisoners of war, while in adjacent camps there were crematoria which Red Cross delegates saw but said nothing about. As international law then stood, the Geneva Convention regime applied only to prisoners of war, and the concentration camp victims were civilian detainees. Accordingly, the ICRC had no formal right under the Convention to visit them. Even so, they might have spoken publicly about what they had seen. They justified their silence with the claim that their access to Allied prisoners would have been suspended had they condemned the treatment of the Jews. As a Swiss organisation, the Red Cross also feared that the price of a public appeal might be German occupation of Switzerland itself. The Red Cross now believes its wartime delegates were mistaken, yet in the Biafran war of 1969–70, its delegates were still ordered to keep silent about evidence that the Nigerians were deliberately using a naval and land blockade of the Biafran region to starve its population into submission, with the active knowledge and connivance of Western powers. This, at least, is what Bernard Kouchner and a number of other French doctors, freshly arrived in Biafra as delegates of the ICRC, believed they were witnessing. It seemed to them – though the subsequent historical record suggests the truth is more equivocal – that, once again, humanitarians were being asked to be silent accomplices to genocide.

With his flair for self-dramatisation, Kouchner says he was born just too late to have been in World War II, 'too late to stop the Holocaust', as he puts it, so he grew up, like most of his generation, in search of a cause equivalent to the French Resistance. His generation included Daniel Cohn-Bendit, leader of the May 1968 demonstrations in Paris, and Regis Debray, who set out to become a guerrilla hero in the mould of Che Guevara and got himself thrown into a Latin American jail. As leftist dreams of revolution died away in the defeat of '68, humanitarianism – noisy, self-promoting and interventionist – took its place. Bernard Kouchner wants you to know that he is the author of that transformation of the European left.

In Biafra, Kouchner, fresh out of medical school and still suffused with the spirit of May '68, led the rebellion against the doctrine of silent neutrality. He ripped off his Red Cross armband, denounced the Nigerian attempt to starve out the Biafrans and later went on to found Medécins Sans Frontières. This rival to the ICRC rejected the politics of humanitarian neutrality and discretion. Its denunciation of rights-violating regimes in the 1970s and 1980s created the new style of humanitarian engagement for NGOs worldwide. The Red Cross remained committed to silent discretion, arguing right through the Bosnian war, for example, that public denunciations of Serbian concentration camps at places like Omarska and Prijedor might make the delegates feel better, but it wouldn't necessarily help the detainees. It might only jeopardise access and the possibility of getting relief through. Medécins Sans Frontières would have none of this. They would denounce what they saw, and if they could not speak honestly about conditions they would not allow themselves to be complicit with evil. This was a noble sentiment, but it came with a cost: it privileged the conscience of the organisation above the claims of victims, and while this might be justified where complicity would compromise the entire integrity of humanitarian action, it might also mean that victims would die because NGOs would not make the political compromises necessary to reach them.

In these debates about the morality of humanitarianism, Kouchner was at the centre, arguing fiercely that humanitarians were not Mother Teresa, saints above politics, but political actors whose very capacity to do good depended on an equal capacity to deal with the devil himself, if necessary, and denounce him publicly if they had to.

Though Kouchner separated angrily from Medécins Sans Frontières more than twenty years ago, when the group won the Nobel Peace Prize, his French critics –

and they are legion – observed sardonically that he behaved as if he had won the prize himself. In a sense, it was true. The Nobel Prize was honouring a new style of politically engaged humanitarian action, and if this new style had a single father, his name was Kouchner.

When Kouchner entered politics, as President Mitterand's minister for humanitarian action, he took the next step in the politicisation of humanitarian action. Aid workers had always seen themselves as free agents, autonomous of the state and rooted in what the jargon refers to as 'civil society'. To be a humanitarian was to rise above the parochialism and moral provincialism of national politics and state interest. It meant a cosmopolitan solidarity, individual by individual, for the poor and suffering of other societies. To be a humanitarian was to be disinterested, and to be disinterested you had to keep a necessary distance from political power, whether exercised by donors, soldiers or diplomats. Humanitarian actors are always talking about a 'humanitarian space', by which they mean a zone in which they can do their work free of political interference from local warlords and from governments back home.

Kouchner was one of those who argued that this attempt to disinfest humanitarianism of politics and state power was an illusion. First of all, most humanitarian organisations depended on state funding for their survival, and while they were entitled to resist government direction and seek to preserve as much humanitarian space as possible, they could not avoid serving at least some of their donor's interests. What mattered was that these interests should be morally defensible, i.e. consistent with basic humanitarian principles. More critically, Kouchner argued, there were some so-called 'humanitarian crises' in the world which were actually political and could only be met by decisive exercises of state power. When Saddam Hussein chased the Kurds into the mountains of northern Iraq in 1991 and murdered as many as he could find with helicopter gunships, the resulting disaster was not a 'humanitarian crisis' at all, but a crime, that could only be answered by creating safe havens for civilians, through the use of Allied air power.

The Kurdish operation in 1991 led Kouchner and others within the Mitterand government to coin the term '*le droit d'ingérance humanitaire*', the right of states to intervene when states oppress their own citizens. At first, Kouchner meant only the right of states to provide humanitarian relief even when the rulers of the violating state – in this case Iraq – refused to give permission. This '*droit d'ingérance*' did not remain a Parisian intellectual abstraction. It certainly influenced French support for the dispatch of UNPROFOR, the ill-fated UN mission in Bosnia, 1992–5, whose function was to deliver humanitarian relief to trapped refugees, encircled populations and cities under siege, like Sarajevo. In Bosnia, Kouchner's humanitarian creed revealed a critical weakness. Humanitarian intervention did not mean stopping the actual fighting. UN peacekeepers were not mandated to break the siege of Sarajevo, stop the bombardment of civilians or prevent ethnic cleansing. The UN troops were only allowed to protect humanitarians seeking to distribute relief to endangered populations. This style of humanitarian intervention met its Waterloo at Srebrenica, where a town full of Muslim refugees trusted to Western promises to provide them security in a safe haven. The Dutch battalion, charged with protecting the civilian population, capitulated to a determined Serbian assault and then stood by as 7,000 Muslim men and boys were taken away and massacred.

The catastrophe of Srebrenica, following the slow martyrdom of Sarajevo, destroyed the credibility of Kouchnerian humanitarian intervention, that is, delivering aid to civilians in the midst of civil war without trying to coerce the belligerents into stopping the fighting. Those who now called for humanitarian intervention after Bosnia meant something completely different: the use of air strikes and ground troops, if necessary, to roll back ethnic aggression, and even to provide military assistance to victims seeking to defend themselves. Traditional humanitarian actors, like the ICRC, were appalled by the way humanitarian motives were being enlisted in defence of military action. But they should not have been surprised. Bosnia had shown that there was no possibility of autonomous, apolitical humanitarian action in the middle of a battlefield. Either you helped one side to win, which was what eventually occurred in August 1995, when the US ordered air strikes against Serb positions in support of a Muslim-Croat advance, or you used humanitarian relief to fatten up populations for slaughter.

Kouchner's own government was as complicit as any other in the unfolding catastrophe of Bosnia. Indeed, it could even be said that his concept of humanitarian intervention legitimised the UNPROFOR operation. His presence in Kosovo, therefore, is full of complex historical irony. More than anyone, he created the model of humanitarian intervention which failed in Bosnia. More than anything, this failure led to Kosovo, where for the first time military means were used to create a humanitarian space for the reconstruction of a country. So, in Kosovo, what Bernard Kouchner represents is the whole tortuous history of modern humanitarianism and its marriage of convenience with state power and military force. The young doctor who began as an insurgent against humanitarian complicity is now the proconsul of an imperial exercise in pacification and nation-building.

It is imperial because it requires imperial means: garrisons of troops and foreign civilian administrators, and because it serves imperial interests: the creation of long-term political stability in the south Balkans, the containment of refugee flows into Western Europe, and the control of crime, drugs and human trafficking. Kouchner knows that the West is not in Kosovo just to feed widows and orphans. Humanitarianism is in the service of long-term state interests of the rich nations on the Security Council who appointed him to his post.

Kouchner also represents something else: humanitarianism's marriage with the media. Since securing TV coverage for efforts to rescue the Vietnamese boat people in the 1970s, no one has done more to use the media to make humanitarianism morally fashionable and economically successful. His most notorious coup was to wade ashore on the beach in Mogadishu in 1992, television cameras rolling, bearing a sack of rice on his back for the starving children of Somalia. His French critics thought the sack of rice was one coup too many, but he insists, to this day, that it was his 'best operation'. Every schoolchild in France gave small packets of rice, and it raised consciousness about Somalia throughout the country.

He claims, with a certain disingenuousness, that he seeks publicity not for himself but for victims. Yet when he says, 'Without photography, massacres would not exist,' he lays bare all that is treacherous in the relation between humanitarianism and the media. For massacres undoubtedly exist without photography. They have a history, context and meaning which is entirely independent of photography and whose deadly logic cannot be captured in images. A culture of compassionate activism that depends on a culture of images cannot hope to grasp all the historical weight and political rationale of the conflicts in which it intervenes. An image-driven humanitarian activism is bound to be shallow. This week's passionate cause will be succeeded by another, and then another. Kouchner himself has cared about so many causes in his life one wonders how he keeps their histories straight. He knows as well as anyone that sustained humanitarian action depends on the kind of solidarity that only comes when people make a claim upon you, face to face. But he also knows that solidarity costs money and money for faraway peoples is not easy to raise unless you can shock people, make them momentarily ashamed. He is a master at making his fellow citizens ashamed, too shrewd not to know that the effect is momentary and must be constantly renewed, with more images, more shocking scenes, more of the soft-core pornography of suffering on which modern humanitarian fund-raising now depends. He also understands politicians, and knows that getting the money depends on making them feel morally uneasy, at least for a moment or two. It is Kouchner, more than anyone else, who created the modern European relation between civic compassion, humanitarian action and the media. Where Kouchner led with Médecins Sans Frontières, all modern humanitarian agencies now follow.

When the French insisted on his candidacy for the Kosovo job, many journalists who had covered the Balkans rolled their eyes in disbelief. Kouchner is one of those politicians whose mastery of the fifteen-minute fame culture seems only to gain the media's contempt. As a government minister in the 1980s and the early 1990s, and as the husband of a beautiful and able television host, Christine Ockrent, he was almost too easy to caricature as '*la gauche caviar*', champagne socialism at its attention-seeking, self-obsessed worst.

Yet those in Priština who predicted he would be on the plane home to Paris every weekend have been proved wrong. 'He lives the job twenty-four hours a day,' says General Klaus Reinhardt, the German who until recently served as the commander of the NATO-led Kosovo force, known as KFOR. 'That's his strength, and also his weakness.' Why weakness? Because he takes everything personally.

'Of course I do,' Kouchner retorts. 'I've been a human rights activist for thirty years, and here I am unable to stop people being massacred.' When UN headquarters in New York insists on calling Kosovo a success Kouchner refuses to use the word. 'Politically, maybe we are a success, but in human rights terms, no.'

In his office in Priština, he shows me a graph of inter-ethnic killings: from a high of about fifty a week in 2001, they have declined to one or two a week. There are more murders in Washington than in Kosovo, Kouchner insists, but he must know that this is beside the point. The

Kosovo killings are political, and they are a direct challenge to the nineteen-nation coalition that intervened in Kosovo to stop ethnic cleansing and finds itself unable to prevent cleansing in reverse.

'Wait a minute,' Kouchner says in his sternest finger-waving style, 'don't deal in false moral equivalencies. The systematic use of Serbian state terror to kill thousands of people and expel nearly a million others from their homes cannot be compared to individual acts of terror, like the bomb placed under the beer van.' True enough, but terror is terror, and its intent is clear: to force the UN and NATO troops to give up their struggle to keep a Serb minority in Kosovo.

Certainly, the ferocity of the hatred in Kosovo took Kouchner by surprise. He arrived in July 1999 talking about European values, tolerance and multiculturalism. By Christmas, as the tide of killings kept rising, he had scaled back his rhetoric of reconciliation. The word he uses now is coexistence. Even that seems a distant goal, with Serbs barricaded in their enclaves, most of the Roma, or Gypsies, still in camps outside Kosovo and only the Kosovars free to walk the streets.

Yet coexistence is not unattainable. It just has nothing to do with any Western ideal of multicultural tolerance. Coexistence means going back to the way Kosovo was between 1974, when Tito gave the Kosovars autonomy, and 1989, when Serbia's Milošević abolished it. In those times, at least if memory is not lying, there were Serbs on one side of the main street in Priština and Kosovar Albanians on the other. One street, two languages, two ways of life. Now there is just one language and one way of life in the cafés of Priština and ordering a beer in Serbian is a distinctly bad idea. When a newly arrived UN official went out into the streets of Priština in the summer of 1999 and having been asked the time replied in Serbian, he paid for his mistake with his life.

Inter-ethnic violence here is having a dampening effect on Western imperial ardour in the region. Already, the UN operation is chronically underfinanced, and Congress keeps talking about pulling Americans out of their huge fortified compound, Camp Bondsteel. But imperial impatience with the locals, the self-serving astonishment at their continuing intolerance, is a piece of bad faith. Why should they conform to our expectations of noble victimhood? Why should they be required to forgive and forget?

Enduring hatred is more than understandable if you go to a village like Celine, among the lush fields that border the road between Prizren and Djakovica. I had been there in the summer of 1999, within a week of the Serb withdrawal. Then the village was deserted and the signs of flight were still evident: mattresses thrown from windows, pathetic trails of dropped shoes, discarded toys left behind in a blind and terrified desire to escape the Serb paramilitaries and police who were going house to house,

64

looting and torching. I followed the trail of discarded clothes and bedding up to a ravine behind the village. There, in a verdant but foul-smelling copse, were the recently exhumed remains of eighteen villagers.

A year later, the roofs are back on the houses; bright zinc drainpipes run down the sides of new brick buildings; the glass is back in the window frames; the children are back in a makeshift school. Up on the hill overlooking the village and the valley, the villagers have buried their dead beneath imposing black granite headstones. Two of them in particular, mixed in with the grown-ups, remain impossible for the village to forgive or forget: Razmazen Ferik Selihu, 1992–1999; Servete Ferik Selihu, 1987–1999.

Children's graves in places like Celine explain why Western sermons about tolerance are met with stony silence among the Kosovar population. There may be as many as five hundred other Celines, mass grave sites where forensic teams from the International Criminal Tribunal at The Hague are still pulling bodies from the ground. Despite revisionist claims to the contrary, original NATO estimates that Serb police and paramilitaries killed more than 10,000 Kosovar Albanians in Kosovo between March and May 1999 will be proved right. The past in Kosovo remains a wound that will not heal.

In the courts that Kouchner has managed to set up, mixed panels of Kosovars, international judges and Serbs are trying the few perpetrators who did not flee to Serbia.

The defendants are charged not with murder but with genocide. While foreign observers, notably Israeli reporters, have been incredulous that there can be a genocide trial with only one named victim and one perpetrator, Kosovars remain convinced that they were all potential victims of a crime against humanity that failed only because both NATO and the KLA came to their defence.

The Kosovars' collective sense of themselves as intended victims of genocide helps to explain the lack of affect with which they tell you, for example, that there had been Serbs in their apartment blocks in Priština but they were all in Serbia now – except, of course, the old lady who had been thrown into her bathtub in her clothes and drowned by a young Albanian couple looking to take over her two rooms. Of course, people regret this crime, even feel shame for it, but there is something else in their eyes as well: indifference.

Kouchner's problem is not just overcoming the cold fury of the Kosovars. There is also the huge obstacle of Serb denial, the refusal to admit either the crimes done in their name or their historical defeat. In Mitrovica, a Kosovo city divided by the Ibar River, the Kosovar Albanians live in the south while the Serbs live in the north. These Mitrovica Serbs, along with those living in other towns north of the river, total 55,000. They are effectively living in Serbia, drawing pensions and salaries from Belgrade, using the dinar rather than the mark and effectively frustrating any attempt by the UN to return Kosovars to the region.

The de facto partition of northern Kosovo, it needs to be said, happened under the very eyes of the French troops sent to secure Mitrovica in the first days after Western entry in June 1999. I was there when it happened, and it was as if the French thought they were in Bosnia, enforcing an UNPROFOR mandate to keep warring factions apart, instead of doing what the Kosovo mandate of the Security Council specifically authorised them to do: occupy the entirety of Kosovo and establish UN authority there. By the time I arrived, Mitrovica was like Mostar in Bosnia, with a bridge dividing two peoples.

The Serb leader there, Oliver Ivanović, is an ingratiatingly fluent English speaker, a former factory manager in his fifties who teaches karate on the side. When NATO rolled into Mitrovica, Ivanović organised his karate class into the 'bridge watchers', the men in dark glasses with walkie-talkies and concealed weapons who guarded the north side of the river and made it impossible for Kosovar Albanians to return to their homes.

Ivanović denies that he is Belgrade's man in Mitrovica. Indeed, he claims to be his own man and insists that Milošević made a mistake in taking on the international community over Kosovo. His job, Ivanović says, is to get the Serbs to cooperate with the internationals. So he will tell you that he can do business with the UN operation in Mitrovica and how he is willing to work with the Kosovar Albanian mayor on the south side of the river. But when he strays from his script and talks about the local zinc and tin mines, the cooperative language fades.

'Look what has happened to the mines since we retreated in 1999,' he says, waving his arms. 'The Albanians have ruined them. They're all flooded. And look at the electricity generators. Now that the Serb managers have left, the power keeps shutting down.' Two decades of Serb underinvestment and neglect are bypassed in an argument that ends, inevitably, with the suggestion that everything would be fine if the old Serb managers were put back in charge.

Besides, Ivanović says, Kouchner is really here to prepare Kosovo for independence. He's not here to protect us. He's here to give the Albanians what they want. When I report this to Kouchner, he shrugs again with fatalistic patience and fingers his worry beads. 'I never talk about independence,' he says. 'It has nothing to do with me. My mandate is purely and simply to prepare Kosovo for substantial autonomy.'

The problem is that 1244, the UN resolution he has been sent here to enforce, is political science fiction. It reaffirms the sovereignty of Yugoslavia over Kosovo, and it also calls for the Kosovars to enjoy 'substantial autonomy and self-government'. This sounds fine, except that no Kosovar will ever accept Belgrade's sovereignty in Kosovo and no Serb in Kosovo wants to accept Kosovar majority rule.

Since everybody on the UN Security Council knows this, the fiction of 1244 must be serving some purpose. First of all, it represents an imperial compromise between the Americans and the Russians. The Russians wish to protect the interests of their client, Serbia, and the Americans are sufficiently distrustful of the Kosovars that they are willing to go along with the Russian fiction that Kosovo should remain under the nominal sovereignty of the Serbs.

This fiction also preserves another appearance: reconciling the imperial exercise of power with the nominal maintenance of the state sovereignty system on which the UN is based. Humanitarian intervention, an imperial exercise of power if ever there was one, is acceptable to other member states of the UN provided that it does not entail the unilateral alteration of sovereign borders. Appearances must be maintained at all costs, even though the entity that is supposed to be sovereign in Kosovo, the Federal Republic of Yugoslavia, is a phantom relic of the Tito era, once six republics in federation, now barely holding together as two, Serbia and Montenegro, and due shortly to disappear altogether. No matter. Even phantoms, apparently, have sovereignty. So Kosovo's future is held in the balance so that appearances of the international state order can be maintained.

But illusions cannot maintain appearances for ever. The larger dilemma that Kosovo illustrates is that once you use imperial power to right human rights abuses you are inevitably set upon a course of altering sovereignty and even altering borders. Despite all the denials by Western governments that humanitarian intervention is becoming the new imperialism, Kosovo does set a precedent. It establishes the principle that states can lose sovereignty over a portion of their territory if they so oppress the majority population there that they rise in revolt and successfully enlist international support for their rebellion. This is not, one should hasten to add, a universal principle. Double standards apply here. America did support the Kosovar struggle for self-determination. It will never support the Chechens against the Russians or the Muslim Uighurs against the Chinese government.

Kosovars also set another kind of precedent. They have proved that violence in a self-determination struggle does pay. Milošević was right: the Kosovars did use terror and violence to secede from Serbia. He was wrong in believing that he could use any means, including attempted genocide and ethnic cleansing, to repress them.

Humanitarian intervention in Kosovo, therefore, was never exactly what it appeared. It was never just an attempt to prevent Milošević from getting away with human rights abuses in Europe's backyard. It was also a use of imperial power to support a self-determination claim by a national minority, a claim that used violence in order to secure international notice and attention.

Kosovo will never return to Serbia: it will be some kind of self-governing entity, even if various fictions are employed, as with Taiwan or Macedonia, to deny it full international statehood. For the moment it is a protectorate, an international legal entity in which nominal sovereignty is exercised by a phantom state, actual sovereignty is exercised by a UN viceroy and day-to-day administration is increasingly exercised by locally elected officials.

All of this is occurring in a deeply divided society with a minority that still believes it is in Serbia and a majority that is prepared to fight, once again, to secure a state of its own. Faced with these divisions, the UN team has focused instead on hard politics – assembling a Kosovo Transitional Council to force the local leaders to sit down together, enrolling voters for elections and helping to draft a blueprint for self-governance. Changing hearts and minds will come later. For now, Kouchner's job is to force Serbs and Kosovars to cooperate, to make them practise Western values, if not at gunpoint, then under the implicit threat that if they don't, the internationals will go and leave them to their Balkan hatreds.

But the threat is a weak one, because most Kosovars understand that the Western troops cannot withdraw without losing face. So the locals have the internationals over a barrel. As a result, the progress of coexistence is agonisingly slow. Kosovars and Serbs sit in Kouchner's large office, a former government headquarters, and they fight over every comma and semicolon. At the end of the meetings, Kouchner's shoulders hurt from the strain of simply keeping victim and victimiser from stalking out. But this is the core of his job: to create political trust where none exists; to create democracy where none has ever taken root before.

Imperial nation-building is politics, and Kouchner is a political animal through and through. He clearly loves the imperial governor side of the job: he bans newspapers when they print the particulars of a Serb employee of the UN whom Kosovar Albanians suspect of being a former ethnic cleanser; he bars a politician from nearby Albania from crossing the border; and in perhaps his boldest stroke, he decides that the mark should become the official currency of the province. He affects not to remember whether he consulted UN headquarters on the currency decision, just so it will be clear that he, and not New York, calls the shots.

His critics often remark, half wistfully, that what the place needs is not a veteran of the human rights movement but a General MacArthur, who rebuilt Japan and implanted a kind of democracy there after 1945. Here, the claim is not that Kouchner is autocratic; it's that he's not autocratic enough and that the UN is too politically

correct, too consultative, too eager to involve local politicians when it should simply lay down the law in classic
imperial fashion.

For example, why bother with courts staffed by local
judges, painstakingly selected from each local ethnic
group, when you could run the whole judicial system with
internationals? Many of those who say this do so not
because they actually want imperial occupation but
because they don't happen to like the Kosovar politicians
– Thaci and Rugova – who benefit from Kouchner's politics of inclusion.

But Kouchner's style is the political style of a whole
generation, including Clinton and Blair, which cannot
exercise power without needing to be loved as well.
Kouchner himself says that he could have been a dictator
in Kosovo but didn't want to be. All the political signals
of his administration are appropriately post-imperialist. As
Jock Covey, Kouchner's American deputy puts it,
'Everything we do here is to work ourselves out of a job.'

But the style is contradictory. In reality, the 'internationals' run everything. Priština's streets are clogged with
the tell-tale white Land Cruisers of the international
administrators, and all the fashionable, hillside villas have
been snapped up by the Western aid agencies, which
number more than 250. The earnest aid workers, with
their laptops, modems, sneakers and T-shirts, all preach
the mantra of 'building local capacity', while the only

discernible capacity being created is the scores of young people who serve as drivers, translators and fixers for the international community. At the political level, the central tension in all nation-building experiments is bubbling to the surface: the conflict between local nationalism and international imperialism; between the desire of local elites to run their own show and the international concern to keep them in leading strings. The question is not who will win – in the end, the locals will win. The question is how long this will take, and how stable Kosovo will be when they take over.

Nation-building in Kosovo does have achievements to celebrate: a whole people returned to their homes and rehoused, the creation of a basic macroeconomic framework, a justice system and the first steps toward institutions of self-government. The process has been agonisingly slow and illustrates all the contradictions of liberal good intentions in a post-imperial era that wants to do good in faraway places without taking up the burdens of a permanent empire.

Right now, however, the auguries are not promising: daily shootings between Serbs and Kosovar Albanians, walkouts on Kouchner's transitional council, the petty feuding among the Kosovar princelings and, above all, the stubbornly unchanging reality of Kosovar backwardness. If you present Kouchner with the evidence that his mission is not succeeding, he does that Gallic shrug and says: 'But of course. You' – meaning the media – 'are only interested in failure. If we were succeeding, you would not be here.' It is not said with a chip on the shoulder, merely with that refusal to pretend otherwise, which makes it possible to believe that this most publicity-seeking of men might not actually be taken in by his own publicity.

Nation-building Lite

The bulky American in combat camouflage, multi-pocket waistcoat, wraparound sunglasses and floppy fishing hat is not going to talk to me. He may be CIA or Special Forces, but either way, I'm not going to find out. These people don't talk to reporters. But in Mazar-e-Sharif, second city of Afghanistan, in this warlords' compound, with a Lexus and an Audi purring in the driveway, armed mujahedin milling by the gate and musclemen standing guard in tight black T-shirts and flak jackets and sporting the latest semi-automatic weapons, the heavy-set American is the one who matters. He comes with a team that includes a forward air controller who can call in air strikes from the big planes doing Daytona 500 loops high in the sky. No one knows how many CIA and Special Forces there are in the country, but the number is small – perhaps as few as 350 all told – but with uplinks to air power and precision weapons, who needs regiments of ground troops? When you ask the carpet sellers in Mazar why there has been peace in the city, they point up into the air. Only America, the carpet sellers say, puts its peace-keepers in the sky.

The biggest warlords in northern Afghanistan, Big D (General Abdul Rashid Dostum) and Teacher Atta (General Ostad Atta Muhammad), are inside this compound, with a United Nations mediator who wants them to pull their tanks back from the city. In Mazar's main square, eyeing one another from the back of their dusty Pajero pickups, equipped with roll bars, fog lights and plastic flowers on the dashboards, are about fifty fighters from each side, fingers on the triggers of rocket-propelled grenade launchers, Kalashnikovs and machine guns. In the past weeks, the militias have been duelling. The fighting has been so bad that the Red Cross hasn't been able to leave Mazar for the central highlands, where as many as 1.2 million people may be starving.

The presence of the American in the warlords' compound is something of a puzzle. George W. Bush ran for the presidency saying he was opposed to using American soldiers for nation-building. The Pentagon doesn't want its warriors turned into cops. Congress is uneasy about American soldiers in open-ended peace-keeping commitments that expose them as terrorist targets. Deep in the background, there still lurks the memory of Vietnam, America's last full-scale attempt at imperial nation-building. But here in Mazar, Americans are once again doing what looks like nation-building:

bringing peace to a city most Americans couldn't have found on a map a year ago.

Yet the Special Forces aren't social workers. They are an imperial detachment, advancing American power and interests in Central Asia. Call it peacekeeping or nation-building, call it what you like, imperial policing is what is going on in Mazar. In fact, America's entire war on terror is an exercise in imperialism. This may come as a shock to Americans, who don't like to think of their country as an empire. But what else can you call America's legions of soldiers, spooks and Special Forces straddling the globe?

These garrisons are by no means temporary. Terror can't be controlled unless order is built in the anarchic zones where terrorists find shelter. In Afghanistan, this means nation-building, creating a state strong enough to keep al-Qaeda from returning. But the Bush administration wants to do this on the cheap, at the lowest level of investment and risk. In Washington they call this nation-building lite. But empires don't come lite. They come heavy, or they do not last. And neither does the peace they are meant to preserve.

Peace in Mazar, it should be understood, is a strictly relative term. The dusty streets are full of turbaned adolescents with Kalashnikovs slung on their shoulders, and firefights are not uncommon. But the American in the floppy hat is not about to call in air strikes to stop a militia shoot-out. He's there to deter the bigger kind of trouble – tank battles or artillery duels. The question is whether the American presence is sufficient to keep Afghanistan from sliding back into civil war. Senators Richard Lugar and Joe Biden have warned that nation-building will fail here unless the force of 4,500 foreign peacekeepers, currently patrolling in Kabul, is expanded and extended to cities like Mazar. They are undoubtedly right, but the Europeans aren't likely to back fine talk with actual soldiers, the Pentagon doesn't want to put peacekeepers on the ground and the Bush administration needs all the legions at its disposal for a potential operation against Iraq. For the time being, it's American peacekeeping in the air or nothing.

In the vacuum where an Afghan state ought to be, there are warlords like Dostum and Atta. They are the chief obstacle to nation-building, but not because they are feudal throwbacks or old-style bandits in uniform. The warlords in the Mazar negotiations are late-modern creations of the American and Soviet duel for influence in Central Asia. Now that the Americans are in the ascendant, each warlord has a press officer who speaks good English and lines up interviews with the foreign press.

They are also building a political constituency at home. Dostum has his own local TV station, and its cameras are in the courtyard waiting to put him on the evening news.

While their power comes out of the barrel of a gun, they also see themselves as businessmen, tax collectors, tribal authorities and clan leaders. Big D actually began life working in the local gas plant. Both he and Teacher Atta prefer to be known as commanders. A warlord, they explain, preys on his people. A commander protects them. Warlords build schools, repair a road or two and make the occasional grand public gesture.

Big D, for example, has placed a plaque near the entrance to the exquisite blue-green sixteenth-century mosque in the centre of Mazar, letting foreign visitors know – in English – that he paid to have the place rewired and the gardens replanted with box hedges and roses. Big D does not attend to the city's more banal needs, like sewers, garbage collection or hospitals. These have languished for twenty-five years. Children with legs ripped apart by mines push themselves along in the dust on home-made carts. But such distress is beneath a warlord's notice. Holding power in Afghanistan is not an exercise in public service.

Nor is Big D's newfound attention to the foreign press a sign of a change of heart. About fifty miles away in Shibarghan – inside a palace decorated with baby pink and blue tiles and surrounded by a rose garden and peacocks – he runs a foul and dilapidated prison where he kept about eight hundred Pakistani Taliban fighters captured in the battle for Kunduz last November. When representatives of the International Committee of the Red Cross visited the prison, they discovered that Dostum was letting the inmates starve to death. These were the lucky ones, it turned out, since thousands of others were shot and pushed into mass graves.

When the local ICRC delegate reminded the general of his responsibilities, Big D denied that he had any. Go talk to President Karzai in Kabul, he growled. The Red Cross had to step in and put the prisoners on an emergency feeding programme like one used in a famine. No sooner had the ICRC restored the prisoners to health than the good general traded them back to the Pakistanis in a gesture of reconciliation. This is how an upper-level warlord plays the new political game in Afghanistan: by forcing international aid agencies to shoulder responsibilities that are actually his own, and then making sure he gets the political credit.

During a break in the negotiations, Big D saunters out into the courtyard. He is a burly figure with short, spiky, salt-and-pepper hair that comes down low above his brows, giving him the appearance of an irritable bear. While his bodyguards take up protective positions around him, he makes calls on the latest in satellite phones, a Thuraya. He's trying to turn himself into a politician, so he dresses like a civilian in a white shirt and slacks. Teacher Atta, when he appears, is wearing a shiny grey suit and carrying a businessman's diary.

Dostum represents Jumbesh, a military and political faction based in the Uzbek ethnic minority, while Atta represents Jamiat, a more religiously flavoured group based among the Tajiks. They are fighting over who will rule Mazar, its blue-green mosque, a population of several million people and a hinterland of well-irrigated fields and some useful natural-gas deposits. But they are also waging a personal vendetta. When I talk to Atta, a tall, gaunt man with deep-set eyes and the intensity of a genuine religious warrior, he says scornfully that while he fought for his country against the Soviet invaders, that low intriguer Dostum was sidling up to the Soviets and keeping out of the fight. As Atta says this, he flicks his white worry beads to and fro like a lion flicking its tail.

Afghanistan has existed as one country since 1919. Although there is a rich heritage of inter-ethnic hatred, most Afghans feel they are Afghans first and Uzbeks, Hazaras, Tajiks or Pashtuns second. This isn't Bosnia, where the country didn't exist until 1992, and Croats and Serbs fought a war to annex their parts of Bosnia to Croatia and Serbia. While the Afghan warlords do get their cash and guns from neighbouring countries like Iran, Pakistan and Uzbekistan, none of them actually want to dismember the country. The warlords don't threaten the cohesion of Afghanistan as a nation. They threaten its existence as a state.

According to the great German sociologist Max Weber, states are institutions that exert a monopoly over the legitimate means of violence in a given territory. By that rule of thumb, there hasn't been a state in Afghanistan since the Soviet Union invaded in 1979 and the war of resistance began. Because the warlords have the guns, they also hold the reins of power. The essence of nation-building is getting the guns out of the warlords' hands and opening up space for political competition free of violence. But this isn't easy in a country where there is no actual difference between a political party and a militia.

It will take years before the national government in Kabul accumulates enough revenue, international prestige and armed force to draw power away from the warlords. But Bosnia shows it can be done. Six years after the war, the Muslim, Croat and Serb armies are rusting away, the old warlords have gone into politics or business and a small national army of Bosnia is slowly coming into existence. The problem in Bosnia is corruption, and that is a better problem to have than war.

In Afghanistan, the Americans are currently beginning training for what they hope will be an 80,000-man army, air force and border police force for the Karzai government. But most of its manpower will come from one ethnic group, the Tajiks from the Panjshir Valley. Unless more Pashtuns, Uzbeks and Hazaras can be recruited quickly, the national army is going to become just another ethnic militia, albeit one financed by the American taxpayer.

While Karzai waits to take charge of his army, his only option with the warlords is to co-opt them, as he has done by appointing Dostum to the grand but empty title of deputy minister of national defence. This means that Dostum's militia is nominally a part of the national army. But on the road between Mazar and Shibarghan, the barracks, tank parks and checkpoints are decorated not with Karzai's picture but with Dostum's. In the north, at least, Karzai looks like nothing more than Mayor of Kabul and vice-president for public relations.

It would be as foolish to be discouraged about this as it would be to suppose that American power can change it quickly. History suggests that nation-building is a slow process. America's own nation-building experience – reconstructing the South after the Civil War – lasted a full century, until the Civil Rights Act of 1964. Overseas, it was the blood and fire of an imposed unconditional surrender in 1945 that enabled America to help rebuild Germany and Japan as liberal democracies. The European states were fully formed to begin with, so the Marshall Plan built on firm foundations. In Bosnia, by contrast, nation-building has been slow because the political institutions left behind by Tito's Yugoslavia were weak. None of the ethnic groups had any experience in making democracy work.

The American capacity to shape outcomes in

Afghanistan, still less to create a state, is constrained by the way it won the war against the Taliban. Its military success in November 2001 was victory lite. The winning strategy paired Special Forces teams and air power with local commanders and their militias. When victory came, America thought it had won the war, but the warlords in the Northern Alliance thought they had. Now they dominate the Kabul government and insist that they, rather than the Americans, should shape the peace.

But even they don't control the Pashtun-dominated south. There, in the valleys and passes bordering Pakistan, nation-building is taking place in the middle of a continuing campaign against al-Qaeda. The only people who know where to find al-Qaeda fighters are the local warlords, and they won't go looking unless the United States pays them handsomely and provides them with weapons. Some Washington policy-makers profess to be untroubled about this: paying the warlords to hunt al-Qaeda keeps them busy, and keeps them under the control of the Special Forces. Yet the essential contradiction in American efforts to stabilise Afghanistan is that in the south, at least, winning the war on terrorism means consolidating the power of the very warlords who are the chief obstacle to state-building.

Moreover, the question of who is using whom is not easy to answer. Ever since the days of the British North-West Frontier, Afghan tribal leaders have been experts at exploiting imperial troops for their own purposes. It's no different now. In December, a southern warlord informed a Special Forces unit that an al-Qaeda detachment was on the road nearby. The detachment was duly hit from the air, only for the Americans to discover that the dead were just some of their warlord's rivals heading off to Kabul. Instead of controlling its warlord proxies, Washington is discovering that it can be manipulated by them.

The parley in the compound at Mazar goes on until seven in the evening. Oncoming darkness concentrates minds – it is not safe, even for warlords, to be on the roads at night, and both Dostum and Atta live outside the city in their own walled enclaves. So at dusk, with the Mazar swallows wheeling in the sky, Big D and Teacher Atta emerge – a deal has obviously been struck – and jump into their black Audi and black Lexus. With their body-guards clambering aboard back-up cars, and the warriors in the Pajero flatbeds falling in behind, the two columns of fighters roar out of the city in a plume of exhaust and dust.

The United Nations negotiators – Mervyn Patterson, a frenetic Northern Irishman, and Jean Arnault, a suave Frenchman – later explain the terms of the deal they have negotiated. 'In the name of Allah, the compassionate and merciful', the document commits the warlords to with-draw their tanks one hundred kilometres from Mazar, to ban heavy weapons and machine guns from the city and to contribute six hundred fighters to form a city police force. The negotiators acknowledge that they have no troops to enforce the deal. But they can call on a powerful friend. Throughout the talks, the American with the floppy hat stood silently in the room.

Imperial presence is the glue that holds Afghan deals together, but there is precious little of it to go around. By comparison, Bosnia, which would fit easily into a couple of Afghanistan's thirty provinces, has 18,000 peace-keepers. But there are none outside Kabul in a country the size of France. The United States wants a presence here, but not an occupation. Afghanistan has been an imperial plaything since the nineteenth century, and nothing makes an Afghan reach for his rifle faster than the presence of an occupying foreign power. So in Mazar, indeed anywhere outside Kabul, the imperial presence is a nebulous thing, a Special Forces detachment here, a plane overhead there.

The day after the deal is done, in the Mazar stadium, a dust-blown space usually used for the chaotic Afghan polo known as buzkashi, six hundred mujahedin, stripped of their Afghan dress and now wearing ill-fitting, hot grey uniforms, straggle out on to the parade ground. As their old militia commanders watch from a shaded viewing stand, sipping cups of tea, the new police force squares off for its first parade. Peace in Afghanistan depends on whether the warlord militias can be lured into policing or other civilian lines of work, and the only people determined to make this transition happen are a silent quartet from Special Forces, watching from the viewing stand, just behind the warlords' adjutants.

Nation-building lite looks too lite in Mazar to be credible for long. Authority relies on awe as much as on force, and where awe is missing, as it was in Mogadishu, Somalia, in 1993, Americans die. The British imperialists understood the power of awe. They governed huge tracts of Africa and populations numbering in the millions, with no more than a couple of administrators for every thousand square miles. In Afghanistan, awe is maintained not by the size of the American presence but by the timeliness and destructiveness of American air power. What the Afghan warlords saw being inflicted on their Taliban opponents, they know can be visited upon them. For the moment, this keeps the peace.

However, awe can be sustained only if force is just – that is, accurate. When American planes pulverised an innocent wedding party, as they did in the summer of 2002, just because some of the more exuberant partygoers were firing into the air, Afghan style, the planners back in Tampa, Florida, will tell you it was just a mistake. But it is more than a mistake: it is a major political error, and the more errors there are, the less awe and the more resistance American power will awaken.

Effective imperial power also requires controlling the subject people's sense of time, convincing them that they will be ruled for ever. The illusion of permanence was one secret of the British Empire's long survival. Empires cannot be maintained and national interests cannot be secured over the long term by a people always looking for the exit.

American power has a reputation for fickleness. CIA agents mysteriously appeared in Afghanistan in the mid-1980s and supplied the mujahedin with Stinger missiles. Once the Soviets were in flight, the Americans went home, leaving Afghanistan to the mercy of the warlords. Years of devastation and war ensued. Afghans have no problem with the idea of a limited American imperial presence, provided that it brings peace and chases away the foreign terrorists from Saudi Arabia, Pakistan and Chechnya. But Afghans look at these American imperialists and wonder, How long will they stay? If, as the rumours go, war against Iraq's Saddam Hussein is next, will the man in the floppy hat with his communications team be here for long?

Back in Kabul, past the Marine security cordon at the fortress-style American Embassy, Elisabeth Kvitashvili, the head of programmes in Afghanistan for the United States Agency for International Development, will remind you bluntly: 'We're not here because of the drought and the famine and the condition of women. We're here

because of 9/11. We're here because of Osama bin Laden.'
USAID had been spending $174 million in Afghanistan
before 9/11, feeding a people abandoned by the Taliban
government. But that figure doubled after 9/11, as
languishing humanitarian motive found itself reinforced
by the national interest of making Afghanistan safe from
terrorism.

In reality, fixing failed states will never guarantee
American security against the risk of terror. Even well-
run states, like Britain and Spain, can find themselves
unwilling harbours for terrorist groups. Rebuilding
Afghanistan's institutions won't necessarily keep al-Qaeda
from creeping back into the country's mountain passes
and caves. Nor will fixing Afghanistan banish terror from
the region. It is just driving al-Qaeda south into the frontier provinces of Pakistan.

Given how difficult it is to police the North-West
Frontier, America will be tempted to declare victory early
and go home. Already, uncertainty about American intentions is causing insecurity. The recent assassination of
Hajji Abdul Qadir, a vice-president and one of the few
ethnic Pashtuns to join the Karzai government, is not just
the normal turbulence of Afghan politics. It is an attempt
to bring down the government, and if it did collapse and
civil wars were to start again, as in 1992, the United States
could not walk away as easily as it did last time. This time
the disgrace would stick. Al-Qaeda would conclude that

if it can topple Karzai, why not topple President Musharraf in Pakistan? Actual defeat, in other words, is a possibility. To avoid it, Washington will have to help Karzai, and the only help that counts in Afghanistan is troops.

Even with American help, the best Karzai and his Kabul government can hope for is to appoint the least bad warlords as civilian governors to keep a rough-and-ready peace and collect some taxes. This sort of ordered anarchy, among loosely controlled regional fiefs, would provide ordinary Afghans with basic security. This may be all that is possible, and it may be all that American interests require. Keeping expectations realistic is the key to staying the course there. Understanding what's at stake is just as important. America could still lose here. If it did, al-Qaeda would secure a victory as large as it achieved on 9/11.

Since the end of the Cold War, nation-building has become a multibillion-dollar business. This is not because rich nations have been seized by a new tenderness of heart towards poor and failing ones. The percentage of Western budgets devoted to foreign aid fell steadily in the post-Cold War period. At a recent conference in Mexico, rich countries promised to do better. But still, with the exception of tiny Denmark, which just scraped by, there isn't a country in the world that devotes even 1 per cent of its gross domestic product to helping poor countries. The United States is nearly at the bottom of the pile, spending a derisory 0.1 per cent of GDP.

Still, small sums eventually add up, and when you figure in all the cheques and credit-card donations from ordinary people flowing into non-governmental development charities, the money for nation-building aid rises into scores of billions of dollars every year. The new mantra of this industry is governance. Economic development is impossible, and humanitarian aid is a waste of time, so the theory goes, unless the country in question has effective governance: rule of law, fire walls against corruption, democracy and a free press. Since most of the countries that need help have none of these things, nation-building programmes to create them have become the chief beneficiaries of government aid budgets.

Nation-building has become the cure of choice for the epidemic of ethnic civil war and state failure that has convulsed the developing world since the end of the long imperial peace of the Cold War. The nation-building caravan has moved from Cambodia in 1993, where the United Nations supervised an election; to Angola, where it failed to secure a peace in 1994; to Sarajevo, where it was supposed to create multi-ethnic democracy; to Priština, where it was supposed to stop the victorious Kosovars from killing all the remaining Serbs; to Dili, in East Timor, where it tried to create a government for a country left devastated by the departing Indonesian militias. Wherever the travelling caravan of nation-builders settles, it creates an instant boom town, living on foreign money and hope. But boom towns inevitably go bust. In Sarajevo, for example, the internationals arrived in 1996 after Dayton with $6 billion to spend. Now, six years later, the money is all but gone, and the caravan is moving on to Kabul.

Kabul is the Klondike of the new century, a place where a young person can make, if not a fortune, then a stellar career riding the tide of international money that is flooding in with every United Nations flight from Islamabad. It's one of the few places where a bright spark just out of college can end up in a job that comes with a servant and a driver. So Kabul has the social attractions of a colonial outpost joined to the feverish excitement of a boom town. But unlike the Klondike, this gold rush is being paid for not by speculators and panhandlers but by rich Western governments.

Empire means big government. One paradox of the new American empire is that it is being constructed by a Republican administration that hates big government. Its way around this contradiction is to get its allies to shoulder the burdens it won't take on itself. In the new imperial division of labour on display in Afghanistan, the Americans do most of the fighting while the Europeans, who don't have ideological problems with big government but don't like fighting, are only too happy to take on the soft sides of nation-building: roads, schools, sanitation and water.

Altogether, rebuilding Afghanistan has been projected to cost between $14 and $18 billion over the next decade. The real figure is certain to be much higher. In Tokyo in January, promises were made of $1.8 billion for reconstruction this year. The Afghans heard the promises. Now they're waiting for the money. In anticipation, Kabul landlords have jacked their rents sky-high – a decent four-bedroom villa that rented for $1,000 a month only a year ago now commands as much as $10,000. In the Kabul bazaars, the booksellers are doing a brisk business in English dictionaries and phrase books. All young Afghans want to learn English, the magic code that opens the door to salaries as drivers, translators, secretaries and cleaners. The car-repair shops, located in rusting freight containers, now hang out hopeful signs – 'Ponctur Repair', 'Fix Foraing Engin' – in the hope of snagging one of the passing white Toyota Land Cruisers. Another sign proclaims 'The Golden Lotos Hotel and Restaurant is Ready Again to Serve You Each Kind of Internal and External Delicious Foods'.

Nation-building isn't supposed to be an exercise in colonialism, but the relationship between the locals and the internationals is inherently colonial. The locals do the translating, cleaning and driving while the internationals do the grand imperial planning. The locals complain that the internationals don't understand anything, not even the local languages. Behind one prominent UN bureaucrat's desk in Kabul there is a furtive crib sheet in Dari, Pashto and English: Stop, Go, Left, Right, Please, Thank You. The internationals may be ignorant – may even arrive believing that the Taliban invented the burka and that women's oppression began with the Taliban seizure of Kabul in 1996 – but ignorance does not stop them from sighing about the corruption, complacency and confusion of the locals.

In nation-building contexts, however, the international lament is complicated by guilt. Every American in Sarajevo knew that his government could have stopped the Bosnian war. In Kabul, everyone knows that the martyrdom of the city, between 1992 and 1996, when duelling warlords reduced large swathes of it to rubble, could have been stopped had the big powers not abandoned Afghanistan after the Soviet withdrawal. So any smart local will exploit international guilt, while any smart international will blame the locals.

These are the colonial continuities in nation-building, but Afghanistan is at least supposed to be different. Such is the gospel according to Lakhdar Brahimi, the wily Algerian diplomat who is the boss of the five hundred-plus UN staff members already in place. Brahimi's engagement with Afghanistan dates back to 1997, when he first tried to broker ceasefires among the warlords. When I ask him what is different this time, he plays with his worry beads and says that all the warlords assure him they have learned a lesson. They don't want to repeat the brutal factional fighting of 1992. But he freely admits that the fighting between Dostum and Atta in Mazar suggests that all the talk of a change of heart may be just talk.

Brahimi has no influence over the American presence in Afghanistan or over its war on terror in the southern provinces. But he worries at the way they are arming warlords in the south. 'I tell the Americans: Why do your planes fly at night here? Because you are afraid of Stinger missiles. And who, may I remind you, brought these missiles to Afghanistan?' Whether Stingers are actually being turned against the Americans, the point remains: if you feed a snake, it may return to bite you.

Brahimi has fought the United Nations bureaucracy in New York to keep the Afghan operation from being flooded with out-of-work nation-builders from the down-sized operations in Kosovo, Bosnia and East Timor. He has also insisted on coordinating the warring UN agencies. 'We want to be sure that the left hand knows what the right hand is doing.' As United Nations boss in Afghanistan, he has resisted playing the role of imperial proconsul, insisting that 'the Afghan government is in the driving seat'.

The theory is that Brahimi's people will force the 'UN family' and what is laughingly called 'the international community' to work in harmony. The reality, as in all nation-building cities, is ferocious competition among donors, United Nations agencies and non-governmental organisations for a market share in money and misery.

The UN nation-builders all repeat the mantra that they are here to 'build capacity' and 'to empower local people'. This is the authentic vocabulary of the new imperialism, only it isn't as new as it sounds. The British called it 'indirect rule'. Local agents ran the day-to-day administration; local potentates exercised some power, while real decisions were made back in imperial capitals. Indirect rule is the pattern in Afghanistan: the illusion of self-government joined to the reality of imperial tutelage.

The white Land Cruisers, the satellite dishes beaming email messages skyward, the banks of computers inside all the UN compounds offer a drastic contrast with Afghan government offices, where groups of men sit around drinking tea, without a computer in sight. At the Afghan Assistance Coordination Authority, the Afghan and international officials trying to coordinate reconstruction believe that as much as $700 million of the money pledged at Tokyo has so far gone to UN agencies, while only $100 million or so has gone to the Afghan administration itself.

The rhetoric about helping Afghanistan stand on its own two feet does not square with the hard interest that each Western government has in financing, not the Afghans, but its own national relief organisations. These fly a nation's flags over some road or school that a politician back home can take credit for. American foreign assistance concentrates on food aid in part because it sops up US farm surpluses. The unpleasant underside of nation-building is that the internationals' first priority is building their own capacity – increasing their budgets and giving themselves good jobs. The last priority is financing the Afghan government.

Admittedly, the capacity of this government is limited. After the new Afghan cabinet ministers came to work in January, there wasn't a fax machine, telephone, desk or chair in their offices until the United Nations shipped them an office kit. Now most of the available chairs are occupied by redundant bureaucrats. The Afghan foreign minister, Abdullah Abdullah, confesses that the only way to get anything done in the ministries is to identify an 'implementation cell' of between five and forty competent people and to pension off the rest.

But the administrative weakness of the Afghan government is also an excuse to keep it enfeebled. How else can a state be created, unless it is given the initial capacity to deliver services and raise its own taxes? It's a colonialist fallacy to suppose that Afghanistan need remain a basket case. Until the Soviet invasion and the civil war that followed, it exported dried fruit, vegetables, precious stones and natural gas. A 'Made in Afghanistan' label could support a big export industry in carpets and luxury clothing. Yet all of these bright prospects will remain a gleam in a few Afghan economists' eyes unless Western governments can provide the Karzai administration with enough operating revenue to get through the first years.

Ashraf Ghani, the worldly and exhausted former World Bank official who is now the government's minister of finance, sits in a wood-panelled office in the prime minister's compound and directs his ire at the condescension of the UN bureaucracy and Western governments. Not a single one of the more than 350 projects submitted by international organisations and NGOs, Ghani says, actually promised to consult the Afghan interim administration. 'This government is asking for accountability,' he says.

Ghani is the most senior example of a trend: the return of the Afghan elite from exile. These returning exiles are not always popular. They are in a hurry, and exile makes them impatient with the old ways at home. Still, the Afghan diaspora, estimated at more than four million people worldwide, is going to be the country's chief source of expertise and investment in the years ahead.

There is growing fury, just visible beneath Ghani's veneer of calm, at the contrast between the international rhetoric of capacity building and the reality of capacity confiscation. How is Afghanistan to build up its own civil service if the government can pay senior officials only $150 a month, while any international NGO or newspaper can pay its drivers $1,000? How can the Afghan government coordinate reconstruction when every day NGOs arrive, fan out into the countryside and find a school to rebuild, an orphanage to establish or an orthopaedic centre to reconstruct, all without telling the Kabul government anything?

Ghani and his staff have put together a national development framework, and in a country where almost everything is broken – roads, schools, agriculture, electric power – it establishes what has to be fixed first. But how do you get foreign agencies to follow the plan, and how do you build accountability between a penniless government and rich donors who don't trust the Afghans to spend it wisely?

Bosnia, Kosovo and East Timor led the internationals to believe that most of the aid that deluges these countries gets siphoned off into corrupt pockets. In Bosnia, the entire criminal and civil justice system was staffed with corrupt leftovers from the Communist era. The internationals ignored this and insisted on early elections, believing that democracy would throw out the crooks. Six years on, Bosnia has had four elections, it still has the same leadership and there hasn't been a single conviction for bribes in a Bosnian court.

This failure to grasp that democracy works only when it goes hand in hand with the rule of law has been the costliest mistake in the Balkans. Instead of creating fire walls against the abuse of power, nation-building exercises usually take the form of funnelling all resources into the hands of a few designated locals whom the internationals deign to trust. When these designated locals begin skimming, the internationals throw up their hands in disillusion. The right strategy, at least if the Balkans is anything to go by, is to build in checks and balances from the start, by helping the Afghans to rewrite the criminal and civil code and train a new generation of lawyers, prosecutors, judges and criminal investigators. Without these legal foundations, no country can make the transition from a war economy to a peace economy.

Currently, the war economy in Afghanistan, the one run by the warlords, depends heavily on the poppy economy. War and drugs will strangle the honest economy if they can't be brought under control. All the money flowing in from international donors and NGOs will sustain the city of Kabul alone and will probably tail off within five years. That leaves the agricultural economy as the backbone of the country: the lovingly irrigated mulberry orchards of Gulbahar, the expanse of vines in the Shamali plain, the rice and wheat fields on the plains between Mazar and Shibarghan. Afghanistan may be a poor country, but there is no reason, if the war and drug economies can be controlled, that it cannot feed itself.

For twenty-five years, Afghan resources have been siphoned into buying weapons. Changing these priorities will take more than turning warlords into politicians. Local revenues will flow to desperately needed projects like rebuilding villages, putting in sewers in towns and collecting the garbage only after ordinary people, especially women, get some way to make their voices heard.

The problem is that most people, especially women, have no institutions of their own. The traditional Afghan jirgas are occasional assemblies convened only for emergencies; the village shura is the preserve of older men and is often dominated by local commanders. Since 1994, Samantha Reynolds, an intense British woman in her thirties who runs the UN's urban regeneration programme, has been convening community forums in urban areas to bring together neighbourhood residents – at first with men and then, as confidence builds, with women as well – to demand basic services, like garbage collection, electricity, sewers and schools. When the municipal officials or local commanders fail to respond, these groups tax themselves to provide them. The Afghan government is currently considering the expansion of the community forums nationwide. They would work out what towns and villages need, apply directly to a World Bank fund and then set about implementing them. It's a grass-roots strategy for building up local leadership, as well as undercutting local commanders and busybody internationals alike.

In the fifties and sixties, thanks to Soviet and American engineers, Afghanistan had some of the best roads in Asia. Nancy Hatch Dupree's old guidebook, published in 1971, and now remaindered on the stalls of Kabul's book market, says that you can get from Kabul to Jalalabad in a couple of hours, and Kabul to Mazar in six. No more. Like those in all failed states, Afghanistan's roads give out when you leave the capital. So does electric power and telephones. It's hard not to think that the place needs fewer humanitarian bureaucrats and more civil and electrical engineers.

All the same, infrastructure cannot create a nation. Bosnia now has the roads and schools it needs, yet its ethnic groups remain as divided as ever. But it's true that Afghanistan won't have a functioning economy until the farmers can get their fruit and vegetables to market and the big truckers from Pakistan and Iran can get goods up to the northern towns. Here the Afghans do need international investment. They can mobilise the construction crews – everybody's idea for weakening the warlords is to create construction jobs for the militiamen – but they need the big lenders to come through with money for the surveys, the engineers and the heavy equipment.

The Afghans are still waiting for delivery on almost all the promises the internationals have made. The overriding fact about reconstruction, at least in the first year, is that the pace set by Afghans has been faster than the internationals can cope with. The United Nations High Commissioner for Refugees expected the refugee return to be rather like it was in Bosnia – slow and cautious. Instead, it came in a flood that overwhelmed its resources. By the end of 2002, an astonishing 1.6 million refugees had returned.

At the beginning, the group was able to provide each family that arrived at its reception centre in Pul-i-Charki, on the outskirts of Kabul, with 150 kilograms of wheat, together with a full medical examination and payment to Pakistani truckers to take them to their villages. Now the big government donors are telling UNHCR that they can't fully finance the programme, and the organisation is cutting back the food ration and the medical assistance.

In March 2002, UNICEF, the UN children's fund, handed every school-age child a plastic bag containing a basic reader, purged of references to guns or warlords, together with a pencil and a writing book. The schools opened, and since then attendance of the school-age population has risen from 5 to 35 per cent. Now, in the hot summer days, by the roadsides, you see files of bare-foot, scrofulous but cheerful children – and girls too – walking to school, carrying their UNICEF bags. But the numbers are not likely to climb above 35 per cent, because donors have given UNICEF only 60 per cent of what it has asked for in its Afghan appeals.

Unless these gaps in financing can be filled, there is going to be trouble. When the refugees get home, they discover that their fields are still full of mines and that the de-miners can't do the work fast enough. The irrigation systems that used to water their fields have been blown up, and the international experts are still walking around doing exploratory studies of how to reconnect them. The villages in the Shamali plain, where the front lines were, are still flattened. So the families camp in the ruins, with their UNHCR tarpaulins as tent material, and try to get a kitchen garden going. Each refugee who returns without a field to till or a home to live in is another potential recruit for the warlords' militias. Afghanistan doesn't need to be on life support for ever, but if it doesn't get sustained assistance for the first three years it may not escape its demons.

Imperialism used to be the white man's burden. This gave it a bad reputation. But imperialism doesn't stop being necessary just because it becomes politically incorrect. Nations sometimes fail, and when they do only outside help – imperial power – can get them back on their feet. Nation-building is the kind of imperialism you get in a human rights era, a time when great powers believe simultaneously in the right of small nations to govern themselves and in their own right to rule the world. Nation-building lite is supposed to reconcile these principles: to safeguard American interests in Central Asia at the lowest possible cost and to give Afghanistan back a stable government of its own choosing. These principles of imperial power and self-determination are not easy to reconcile. The empire wants quick results, at the lowest possible cost. That means an early exit. The Afghans want us to protect them, and at the same time help them back on their feet. That means sticking around for a while.

Washington had better decide what it wants. If it won't sustain and increase its military presence here, the other internationals will start heading for the exit. If that occurs, there is little to stop Afghanistan from becoming, once again, the terror and heroin capital of the world. There is no reason that this needs to happen. Afghans themselves know they have only one more chance. They understand the difficult truth that their best hope for freedom lies in a temporary experience of imperial rule.

They are ready to seize the moment. It is easy to be cynical about the imperial outsiders, however necessary they may be, but it is hard not to be moved by the Afghans themselves. The nation-builders to bet on are those refugee families, piled on to the brightly painted Pakistani trucks, moving up the dusty roads, the children perched on the mattresses, like Mowgli astride the head of an elephant, gazing towards home.

The nation-builders to invest in are the teachers, especially the women who taught girls in secret during the Taliban years. I met one in an open-air school right in the middle of Kabul's most destroyed neighbourhood. She wrote her name in a firm, bold hand in my notebook, and she knew exactly what she needed: chalk, blackboards, desks, a roof and, God willing, a generation of peace. At her feet, on squares of UNHCR sheeting, sat her class, twenty upturned faces, all female, having the first reading lesson of their lives.

Finally, you could believe in the brick-maker, alone with his five-year-old son, in the middle of an expanse of desolate ruins in downtown Kabul. After the militia fighting in 1992, nobody bothered to make bricks. What was the point? The shelling might start all over again. But now the brick-maker had his wooden form in his hands, pressing it down into a mixture of straw and mud that has served to make bricks since the time of the Prophet. Behind him, a hundred neat brown bricks were drying in the last dusty light of the day. The brick-maker had a beard, a dirty kaftan and a cap on his head. All he had ever known was war. When I asked him why he thought it was time to make bricks again, he said: 'We have a government now. People need houses.' He didn't have time to talk more. He was too busy making bricks.

It would be too much to say that the brick-maker wants us infidels here, exactly, but I would venture that he knows he needs us. With us here he is able to gamble. But without the Americans in floppy hats nobody is going to feel safe enough to start building a house with his bricks.

Conclusion: Empire
and its Nemesis

These three tales from the frontier all describe a new exercise of imperial rule. Imperial is the word to use even if these border zones are not going to be occupied in perpetuity and ruled as colonies. Bosnia and Afghanistan are supposed to be independent states, and Kosovo is being prepared for an independent future. Yet all three are on life support, dependent for their survival on foreign troops, international aid and diplomatic protection from the great powers. The nation-building enterprise pursued in all three is imperial because its essential purpose is to create order in border zones essential to the security of great powers – and because armed force, an instrument only great powers can use with impunity, is critical to the task. It is imperial, finally, because while nominal power may return to the local capital – Kabul, Sarajevo and Priština – real power will continue to be exercised from London, Washington and Paris.

The imperial design needs to be stressed, because the usual way of describing Bosnia, Kosovo and Afghanistan, as wards of the 'international community', obscures the imperial interests that brought them under the administration of the United Nations in the first place. None of the three cases would have been chosen as a suitable case for humanitarian treatment had they not also been a practical venue for the exercise of military force by the United States.

In the case of Kosovo and Bosnia, the rationale of imperial self-interest found additional support from the language of human rights. The troops were sent there not just to restore order but to protect people from ethnic cleansing and massacre. In the case of Afghanistan, human rights played a secondary role: if intervention could improve the condition of Afghan women, so much the better, but no one seriously pretended that was the motive for the American campaign. Afghanistan became an object of intervention only when it became a strategic threat.

To the extent that human rights justify the humanitarian use of military force, the new empire can claim that it serves the cause of moral universalism. Yet its service to the cause is equivocal. If America were consistent about defending human rights everywhere, it would have to dispatch marines to every failed or failing state where populations are threatened with massacre or genocide. Doing so would be both vain and unwise. Empires that

110

are successful learn to ration their service to moral principle to the few strategic zones where the defence of principle is simultaneously the defence of a vital interest, and
where the risks do not outweigh the benefits. This is why
modern imperial ethics can only be hypocritical. The new
imperium has been imposed in the Balkans but it is never
going to be extended to Chechnya. It will be created in
Afghanistan but never in Chinese Central Asia. America
will not risk military confrontation with Russia or China
simply because the human rights of their subject populations are at risk. Yet hypocrisy and cynicism are not iden-
tical. The fact that empires cannot practise what they
preach does not mean that they do not *believe* what they
preach. The problem is not the sincerity or otherwise of
their beliefs, but the impossibility of always putting them
into practice. Those who regard imperial attachment to
human rights as entirely cynical might ask themselves
what price consistency? Is it worth pursuing at the risk of
a confrontation with nuclear powers? This is not an
apologia for silence in the face of Russian or Chinese
tyranny, but rather an acknowledgement that, in these
cases, the pressure will have to avoid the threat of force.
Because American force cannot be used where there is
risk of defeat or serious casualties, the redemptive exercise of temporary imperial rule is sure to be practised only
where it is safe to do so, where the costs, in advance, are
known to be worth the risk.

New technologies of precision air power, surveillance satellites and logistics have helped to bring these costs down. It is possible to garrison Afghanistan with thousands rather than tens of thousands of troops as in the past, and rapid communications ensure that these garrisons can be resupplied before they meet the fate of the British expeditions in Afghanistan in the 1840s who were cut apart by Afghan tribesmen while London continued in blithe ignorance of their fate. Thanks to technology, American imperialism can now combine a light footprint on the ground with lethal coverage from the air.

Because the Americans have a near monopoly on these technologies, together with unrivalled military power, their interests dominate the condominium of Western states that have put the new imperium in place. Japan and the European Union play an important role as paymasters, but if American power withdraws from any of these places, nation-building cannot be sustained. So this is not a new *American* empire, since other Western powers have formidable stakes in the success of the enterprise, especially in the Balkans, but it is American in its leadership, and without its leadership the new imperium will founder.

As an empire run by Western liberal democracies, chiefly America, its moral grace notes are all liberal and democratic. Its purpose is to extend free elections, rule of law, democratic self-government to peoples who have only known fratricide. In the process, Western nations have learned something about themselves, namely that democracy means little if it is not buttressed by separation of powers, an independent judiciary and the rule of law. Democracy without these constitutional supports just provides an opportunity for populist tyranny and financial corruption. In the Balkans, nation-builders learned that giving people the vote was not the same as giving them self-rule. Nation-building means building a constitutional order, the rule of law rather than the rule of men, and this is difficult in societies that have only known the latter.

This is not the only discovery. Achieving democratic goals through imperial means is, of course, an exercise in contradiction. A true democracy cannot be ruled by foreigners. The new imperium of UN administrators, backed by foreign troops, has sought to resolve these contradictions by means of a pre-set exit timetable. The outsiders force the pace of elections and legal reform by announcing, beforehand, the date of their departure. The imperial system both rewards and punishes: if you behave, you will be masters in your own house; if you don't, we will abandon you to your warlords.

Empires in times past, the Romans for example, made permanence the basis of their capacity to enforce obedience. The rule was: we will never be intimidated into leaving, so you have no choice but to obey. By contrast, all modern imperial rule is temporary, justified as the exercise of force and coercion necessary to restore peoples to their sovereignty. As we have seen from these tales from the frontier zone, managing this essential contradiction is the whole art of the modern imperium: building institutions for the sake of local people, without confiscating their decision-making capacity; forcing them to take responsibility without abandoning them to the demons of their past.

It would be a mistake to assume that these dilemmas are entirely new. Ruling peoples, with a view to preparing them for self-government, is a very old function of empire. The British began preparing their white colonies for self-government in the 1840s, and even when Canada became a self-governing dominion in 1867, it remained a part of the British Empire. When Canadians went overseas to do battle at the Somme in 1916, they fought for King and Country. Few soldiers saw any contradiction between being a citizen and being a subject. Imperial and civic identities were intertwined in a single patriotism.

What the history of the British Empire shows is that self-determination and imperial rule are not incompatible. Indeed, promising self-government has always served as a key instrument in maintaining control. When the British took Palestine under the League of Nations mandate, after driving the Ottomans out of the Middle East during World War I, the rationale of British colonial administration was to prepare two peoples, Arabs and Jews, for some kind of self-government, preferably under continued British jurisdiction. The justification of mandate rule was not very different from the protectorate's purpose in Kosovo. The only element that may be new is the time factor. The British gave themselves two generations in Palestine – and also in India – before throwing up their hands in despair. The timetable for Kosovo and Bosnia is considerably shorter. They must make the transition from war to peace, from Communist political culture to Western democracy, in less than a decade. Afghanistan will be force-marched towards democratic elections within three years. No imperialists have ever been so impatient for quick results.

This impatience has complex roots – the short attention span of modern media, the competing interests of the condominium of powers who pay for these imperial exercises – but the central factor has to be the democratic character of the Western powers. Most empires of the past were not democracies at home, and they did not aspire to make their colonies democratic abroad. Autocratic forms of rule at home helped to maintain long-term continuities in imperial rule abroad. Democratic empire is short-term. The political timetables imposed on Bosnia, Kosovo and Afghanistan are dependent on the electoral cycle back home. No modern incumbent wants to be saddled with an imperial failure in an election year, especially when faced with a challenger who is calling for the troops to come home. These electoral pressures help explain the fixation with quick results and exit timetables. These new empires depend, ultimately, on the staying power of electorates, and democratic peoples make fickle imperialists, not always sure that the game is worth the candle. Who would not rather have a hospital built next door than 10,000 miles away for some foreigners? The impulses that sustain humanitarian reconstruction have to compete with domestic priorities and it takes a determined exercise of leadership to convince people that expenditure on nation-building is necessary for their security. The American people, secure within a continental nation state, have never been certain that their security requires the permanent garrisoning of their sons and daughters overseas. They lent reluctant support to the imperial project of the Cold War proposed to them by the East Coast foreign policy elites. Over Vietnam, this reluctant alliance between the public and its foreign policy elites broke down completely. With their sons dying abroad and with no end in sight, the American public, or at least a sizeable minority of it, finally rose up in revolt and forced the empire into its first and only retreat.

Vietnam remains the ghost at the American imperial feast, the one enduring lesson it has ever learned in hubris. For here was a road to hell surely paved with good intentions. Vietnam was an imperial nation-building project, an attempt to use military power to sustain a democratic republic in South Vietnam against what seemed like foreign, Communist and anti-democratic incursion from the north. Like Afghanistan, Bosnia and Kosovo, Vietnam was understood at the time as a noble cause, in which Americans put technology and will in the service of the South Vietnamese right to self-determination. That it was also a crude, unilateral exercise in imperial self-interest – holding back the Communist advance into Asia – should not obscure the moral appeal of the project to the young Americans who went to Saigon in the early 1960s, as young Americans go to Sarajevo, Priština and Kabul in this century.

What defeated the Americans in Vietnam, among many other things, was a failure to understand that liberal good intentions, even when equipped with helicopter gunships, are no match for the aroused power of modern nationalism. Vietnam was a titanic clash between two nation-building strategies, the Americans in support of the South Vietnamese versus the Communists in the north. It proved impossible for foreigners to build stability in a divided country, against resistance from a Communist elite fighting in the name of the Vietnamese nation. Vietnam is now one country, ruthlessly consolidated under an authoritarian leadership, but its civil war is over and its long-term stability is assured. The Vietnam case shows that nationalism will always prove to be the nemesis of any imperial nation-building project.

The post-Vietnam problem – the one for which temporary empire remains a solution – is that for every Vietnam, for every successful nationalist nation-building venture, there are countless others which have ended in war, chaos and disorder. The Balkan wars of the 1990s were a clash of nation-building elites, all struggling to build nations on the ruins of the Yugoslavia Tito had left behind. Had Greater Serbia and Greater Croatia succeeded, for example, in carving out their own states on the corpse of Bosnia, the great powers might never have intervened. It was because these nation-building wars ended in catastrophic stalemate that foreign power had to come in to impose an imperial nation-building process of their own.

Afghanistan is a more complex example of the way in which failed attempts at nation-building make imperial interventions necessary. For after the civil war of the 1990s, the Taliban did succeed at nation-building of a sort. They conquered and established an order of a kind throughout all but 10–15 per cent of the country between 1996 and 2000. Here religion, rather than nationalism alone, provided the cement for nation-building. While Western governments would now prefer to forget this period, they did welcome the Taliban as nation-builders of a sort: they were divided between distaste for the Taliban's domestic repression and relief that the Afghan civil war seemed all but over. In those years, the US placed a double bet, continuing to provide minimal levels of support for the Afghan opposition, while leaving the Pakistan secret service a free hand to support the Taliban. September 11 exposed the policy as a catastrophe. America had covertly supported a Pakistani-inspired nation-building exercise, but the nation they built turned out to be a training ground for barbarians. The nation that emerged fell hostage to al-Qaeda, the revolutionary foreigners who came as guests and stayed to become paymasters and controllers of the Taliban state. The empire had to beat the barbarians back and start nation-building all over again.

But empire will not succeed if it thwarts and represses the forces of Afghan nationalism, both religious and secular. As Vietnam shows, imperial force is no match for a people with nothing to lose. Afghanistan may be a failed state, but the balance of will between local people and internationals is more even than the imbalance of their resources may suggest. Condescension towards Afghan capabilities and capacities is more than unworthy: it may only engender revenge. The Afghan people know they have seen off two empires, the British and the Russian. There is no reason why they cannot see off a third.

America's leadership role in the reconstruction of failed states is also full of ironies. Its status as the sole remaining imperial power makes it easy to forget how much of its international prestige in the twentieth century derived from taking the side of freedom against empire. At the

Versailles Conference of 1919, the American president made himself the champion of the principle of self-determination. It was American leadership that led to the dissolution of three empires – the Ottoman, Romanov and Habsburg – and the granting of national political freedom to the peoples of Eastern and Southern Europe.

After World War II, the same principle of self-determination inspired the revolt of African and Asian peoples against colonial domination. First the Dutch empire in Indonesia, then the French empire in Indo-China and North Africa, and then the British and Belgian empires in Africa fell to colonialist uprisings and colonial self-disillusion. Although not directly involved, the United States watched the death agonies of the European empires with satisfaction and profited directly from their demise. As a republic founded in revolt against a European empire, it sought influence with former European colonies by portraying itself as the world's most successful example of an anti-colonial uprising.

Europe's imperial retreat after World War II gave America its imperial opportunity. During the Cold War, it built an empire to combat an imperial rival and protect its allies. Again, the organising ideology of the American struggle against Communist expansion was self-determination. Its proclaimed aim was to free the captive nations from the Soviet yoke. With the end of the Cold War, and the collapse of the Soviet Union, the last of the great

Conclusion: Empire and its Nemesis

European empires released its grip on the peoples of Eastern Europe and Asia. America emerged as the sole remaining imperial guarantor, yet the paradox of its rise to power has been the way it has associated its international prestige with anti-imperial premises. At least this was true in Europe and Asia. In Latin America, in the zone it regarded as its backyard, American respect for self-determination was less obvious. Legitimately elected governments were overthrown, and undemocratic regimes were sustained against the wishes of their people so that American power could rule unopposed in its hemisphere. Where imperial interests and self-determination conflicted, imperial interests prevailed.

Self-determination was not the only driving impulse of anti-colonial revolt after World War II. The European empires had justified the white man's burden with theories of their own racial and cultural superiority. Imperial authority was justified as a necessary stage of tutelage in which lesser breeds learned the habits of mind necessary for self-rule. Condescension sustained the imperial project, but also doomed it. The nemesis of empire was not just nationalism, but narcissism: the incorrigible self-satisfaction of imperial elites, their belief that all the variety of the world's peoples aspired to nothing else but to be a version of themselves.

The titanic anti-colonial figures of the twentieth century – from Gandhi to Mandela – succeeded in making the idea of self-determination and the idea of human equality triumph over the imperial idea of racial hierarchy. America's own reckoning with the heritage of white superiority came at home in the civil rights struggles of the 1950s and 1960s. Martin Luther King can be seen as the American voice of a global movement against empire and its injustice.

The core beliefs of our time are the creations of these anti-colonial struggles: the idea that all human beings are equal, and that each human group has a right to rule themselves free of foreign interference.

It is at least ironic that liberal believers in these ideas – someone like me, for example – can end up supporting the creation of a new humanitarian empire, a new form of colonial tutelage for the peoples of Kosovo, Bosnia and Afghanistan. The reason simply is that, however right these principles may be, the political form in which they are realised – the nationalist nation-building project – so often fails to deliver them. For every nationalist struggle that succeeds in giving its people self-determination and dignity, there are more that only deliver their people up to a self-immolating slaughter, terror, enforced partition and failure. For every Vietnam successfully created by nationalist struggle, there is a Sierra Leone or Somalia dying of institutional collapse and civil war. For every South Africa that achieves majority rule, there is a Palestinian struggle trapped in a downward spiral of terror and military oppression.

Conclusion: Empire and its Nemesis

The moral premises of anti-imperialist struggles in this century – all peoples should be equal, and all peoples should rule themselves – are not wrong. But history is not a morality tale. The age of empire ought to have been succeeded by an age of independent, equal and self-governing nation states. In reality, it has been succeeded by an age of ethnic cleansing and state failure. This is the context in which the empire has made its return. Empire is an attempted solution to the crisis of state order that has followed two botched decolonisations: the Soviet exit from Europe, and the European exit from Africa and Asia. This crisis of state order is not confined to the Balkans or Afghanistan. The phenomenon is global. From Colombia in Latin America, to Sierra Leone in West Africa, from Somalia in East Africa, to Indonesia, a set of fifteen to twenty states is struggling to contain domestic insurrections, liberation struggles by repressed minorities, or the advanced decay of the state structures they inherited from colonial powers at independence.

This does not mean all post-independence colonial states have failed or are likely to do so. For every Sierra Leone or Somalia, there is a Mozambique or a Bangladesh, making government work in a poor and adverse environment. It does not mean that all the states created out of the collapse of the Soviet empire are failing either. For every Ukraine, there is also a Hungary. For every Moldova, there is a Lithuania.

Yet there is enough failure to create an ongoing crisis of order in a globalised world. For thirty years after decolonisation this crisis has grown upon us, and all the rich Western world has done is to pretend it is not occurring. First, we believed in the theology of development, only to see development founder on corruption and the incapacity of weak state structures to develop honest government and equitable programmes for growth. Then we told ourselves globalisation itself – capitalism's sheer voracious dynamism – would bring prosperity and order in its wake. But markets alone cannot *create* order: markets *require* order if they are to function efficiently, and the only reliable provider of order – law, procedure, safety and security – is the state. A globalised economy cannot function without this structure of authority and coercive power, and where it breaks down markets break down, and crime, chaos and terror take root in the rotten, unpoliced interstices. Prophets of the benefits of global market integration have been foolish enough to envisage a future world that does away with the need for the state. But large corporations will not patrol the street corners. They will not provide the schools, roads and hospitals that distinguish society from the jungle. Only states can provide these goods. Authoritarian forms of rule can do so, but only states chosen by their people and governed according to the rule of law can do so in conditions that are likely to be stable, secure and at peace with their neighbours.

124

Conclusion: Empire and its Nemesis

The larger global reality is that the American ascendancy in the twenty-first century happens to have coincided with the disintegration of some of the states in Africa and Asia who won their independence from the previous colonial rulers, and the disintegration of the states that won their freedom from the Soviet empire in 1991. This is the larger context that helps to explain why the new imperial project – consolidating zones of stability in areas of vital national interest – is proving necessary. The imperial problem is much larger than Afghanistan, Bosnia or Kosovo. Nothing less than the reconstitution of a global order of stable nation states is required. This is beyond the power of even the greatest empire. Yet these nations, by themselves, cannot heal their own wounds, self-inflicted or otherwise. It is a delusion, even for those who believe fervently in the equality of peoples and their right to rule themselves, to believe that they can always succeed in nation-building on their own. Those who imagine a world beyond empire imagine rightly, but they have not seen how prostrate societies actually are when nation-building fails, when civil war has torn them apart. Then and only then is there a case for temporary imperial rule, to provide the force and will necessary to bring order out of chaos. The problem is that the number of societies in this condition exceeds the force and will of peoples with the capacity for empire. So these societies will have to create themselves, and the instrument they commonly use to do so is war. War has always been the mother of nations. The globe is experiencing what Europe lived through in the Hundred Years War, a bloody struggle to consolidate the state order without which liberty is impossible. In the end there cannot be order in the world, and certainly no justice, without democratic self-rule. Every people need not have a state, but people must rule themselves. But to reach that destination, the peoples who do not rule themselves will have to struggle, and while empire can help, repress and contain the struggle, it cannot control it. Only a very deluded imperialist would believe otherwise.

If this is so, empire's strategy should be to contain and channel the explosive force of modern nationalism rather than fight it as in Vietnam. In the three de facto protectorates of Kosovo, Bosnia and Afghanistan, the strategy must be to force responsibility on to local elites, rather than trying to hold onto it itself. Imperial power should be used to keep these zones free of external interference and aggression as well as internal civil war. But it must be the local political authorities who rule in fact as well as name. At the moment, empire lite does neither: it neither provides a stable long-term security guarantee, nor creates the conditions under which local leadership takes over. Everything is done on the cheap, from day to day, without the long-term security guarantees and short-term financial assistance that would genuinely create the conditions for true national independence. To exercise power in this way is to risk losing authority, and to risk losing everything eventually, since peoples disillusioned with our promises will have enduring reasons never to trust us again.

Index

EMPIRE LITE

130

Index

Index